Anáil Dé:
The Breath of God

Music, Ritual and Spirituality

Edited by Helen Phelan

VERITAS

Published 2001 by
Veritas Publications
7/8 Lower Abbey Street
Dublin 1
Ireland

Email publications@veritas.ie
Website www.veritas.ie

ISBN 1 85390 597 6

British Library Cataloguing
in Publication Data.
A catalogue record for
this book is available
from the British Library.

Cover design by Bill Bolger
Printed in the Republic of Ireland by Betaprint Ltd, Dublin

Veritas books are printed on paper made from the wood pulp of managed forests. For every tree felled, at least one tree is planted, thereby renewing natural resources.

CONTENTS

CONTRIBUTORS

Ioannis Arvanitis studied Byzantine music in the Odeion of Halkis and acquired his diploma for teaching Byzantine music from the Skalkotas Music School with Lykourgos Angelopoulos. He currently teaches in the Ionian University and in the Odeion Philippos Nakas. He is an international performer of Byzantine chant and has a specialist interest in its theory and palaeography.

Barra Boydell is senior lecturer in music at the National University of Ireland, Maynooth. His major research interest is the history of music in Ireland. The author of a number of books, including *Music at Christ Church before 1800: documents and selected anthems* (Dublin, 1998), he wrote the chapters on music for *Christ Church Cathedral Dublin: a History* (ed. by K. Milne, Dublin, 2000) and is a contributor to the *Revised New Grove* and *Die Musik in Geschichte und Gegenwart*.

Chartwell Dutiro started playing *mbira* at the age of four for spirit mediums at *bira* ceremonies in his home country of Zimbabwe. He currently lives in London and plays in his own group, Spirit Talk Mbira. He teaches at the School of Oriental and African Studies, London University, where he is also reading a PhD.

Gerard Gillen is Professor of Music at the National University of Ireland, Maynooth, and co-editor of *Irish Musical Studies*. He is chair of the Roman Catholic Bishops' Advisory Committee on Church Music and Titular Organist of Dublin's Pro-cathedral.

Ronald Grimes is Professor of Religion and Culture at Wilfrid Laurier University in Ontario, Canada. His publications include *Marrying and Burying: Rites of Passage in a Man's Life* and *Deeply into the Bone: Re-Inventing Rites of Passage*. He is editor of *Readings in Ritual Studies*.

C. Michael Hawn is Associate Professor of Church Music at Perkins School of Theology, Southern Methodist University. In addition to teaching, he has served churches in Kentucky, Georgia, North Carolina and Texas as minister of music. He holds the Doctor of Musical Arts and the Master of Church Music degrees from Southern Baptist Theological Seminary, Louisville, Kentucky

Mark Patrick Hederman OSB has been a monk of Glenstal Abbey in Limerick for over thirty years. Formerly headmaster of the school, and currently academic dean, he did his doctorate in the philosophy of education. He studied in Paris under Emmanual Levinas. He has lectured in philosophy and literature in America, Nigeria as well as Ireland, and was a founding editor of the cultural journal *The Crane Bag*. Recent publications include *Kissing the Dark* (Veritas, 1999) and *Manikon Eros: Mad, Crazy Love* (Veritas, 2000).

Kaja Jensen is Head of Music Therapy at Southern Methodist University in Dallas, Texas, and has worked as a music therapist and music therapy educator since 1979. She has worked and trained students in a variety of psychiatric, medical, geriatric, developmental, correctional and intermediate care facilities. Her research interests include the use of music in psychotherapy and the derivation of emotion and meaning in music.

Rachel Levay is an international music festival organiser and project developer and has worked all over the world with the WOMAD Festival organisation. She is currently reading an MMus at the School of Oriental and African Studies, London University.

Katarina Livljanic is a Croatian singer and musicologist. She has studied voice with Marie Noël Colette and Brigitte Lesne, and obtained her PhD at the École Pratique des Hautes Études in Paris based on research of medieval chant manuscripts of Southern Italy. She directs a vocal ensemble Dialogos, specialising in medieval chant and liturgical theatre, and currently teaches at the Parisian Sorbonne University

Cyprian Love OSB is a monk of Glenstal Abbey, County Limerick. He holds degrees in theology and music from the Universities of London and Hull. A fellow of the Royal College of Organists, he has made two CD recordings on the organ at Glenstal Abbey, one including Tournemire's transcribed improvisation on the *Te Deum* and *Cantalène Improvisée;* another consisting mainly of his own improvising, entitled *Dancing Before the Ark.*

Fintan Lyons OSB taught ecumenical studies at the Pontifical Liturgical Institute, Rome, until 2000 when he was recalled by his community to serve as novice master at Glenstal Abbey. He is a member of the Pentecostal-Roman Catholic International Dialogue, and publishes regularly on ecumenical and other theological topics.

Noirín Ní Riain is an internationally acclaimed spiritual singer and has performed and recorded extensively. She is author of three books and several articles including recent contributions to three major publications from Women's Press, London, Quarry Music Books, Canada, and COMECE publications, Brussels. She was Artist-in-Residence with Laois County Council in 1999, the first ever singer to be appointed to such a position. She is currently pursuing a doctoral degree in theology and is the recipient of a doctoral scholarship from the University of Limerick.

Seán Ó Duinn OSB is a Benedictine monk and priest of Glenstal Abbey. He lectures in Irish Heritage Studies in Mary Immaculate College, University of Limerick. His published works include *Orthaí Cosanta sa Chráifeacht Cheilteach,* a research work on the 'Protection prayer' tradition and a new edition of the ancient Irish saga, *Forbhais Droma Dámhgháire, The Siege of Knocklong.* His doctoral thesis is on 'The Rites of Brigid-the-Goddess and the Saint'.

Mícheál Ó Súilleabháin is Professor of Music at the University of Limerick where he established the Irish World Music Centre in 1994 for the purpose of research and performance in Irish and Irish-related music worldwide. He is well known for his development of a unique piano style and for orchestral compositions and arrangements that blend Irish and classical sounds within a world music context. His recordings include *The Dolphin's Way, Oileán/Island, Casadh/Turning, Gaiseadh/Flowing, Lumen, Between Worlds, Irish Destiny* and *Becoming.*

Helen Phelan is a lecturer in liturgical music at the Irish World Music Centre, University of Limerick, and course director of the Masters programme in Chant and Ritual Song. She is director of *Anáil Dé,* an annual Festival of Sacred World Music in Limerick. Her doctoral research explored the emergence of a theology of music with reference to Irish Catholicism.

INTRODUCTION

Helen Phelan

THE IMPULSE TOWARDS RITUAL is strangely animal, human and spiritual. The exorbitant, exuberant plumage of birds and their ritualised mating dances, as well as the territorial battles and ritual games surrounding the mating practices of many species, remind us that ritual is often linked to the most basic survival behaviours of procreation and reproduction.

For the human species, ritual has developed to include not just the ability to survive physically, but to engage with the existential questions of why we exist and how we survive this existence with humanity. In *The Farewell Symphony*, Edmund White charts the story of the American gay community in the early generations of AIDS and its attempt to live with the unremitting deaths of lovers, brothers, sons, friends and entire communities. Often disenfranchised from institutional religion, the survivors found themselves creating ritual out of necessity and instinct. White concludes that, 'death without rituals is intolerable',[1] echoing the sentiments of Antigone in Sophocles' famous tragedy:

> No, I do not suffer from the fact of death.
> But if I had let my own brother stay unburied
> I would have suffered all the pain I do not feel now.
> And if you decide what I did was foolish,
> You may be fool enough to convict me too.[2]

Individuals and societies often play out their grapplings with life's meaning through the drama of ritual. In his novel, *Lie Down in Darkness*, William Styron uses the marriage of a child – 'no ceremony

in the Christian culture is more exciting or awe-inspiring than a
wedding'[3] – as the stage upon which various characters will struggle
to come to terms with the web of events that have created their life's
journey. Similarly, Japanese author and Nobel laureate Kenzaburo Oe
creates the monster 'Chosokabe', who fills up all time and space and
acts as a metaphor for history. Influenced by the Romanian scholar
of myth and religion, Mircea Eliade, Oe's depiction of the world
reveals cosmic waves of annihilation and purification of history (the
monster) through life's own ritual repetitions.[4]

The jump from existential to spiritual ritual should not surprise
us, as spirituality has developed as an existential anchor across time,
culture and geography. Spirituality and religion provide meaning,
which ritual enacts and encodes. Through its deep store of music,
holy texts and stories, costume, vestment, gesture, space and smell,
spiritual or religious ritual conjures up a voice beyond voice, allowing
a glimpse into the invisible, inaudible secrets of why we are here and
what it means to be alive.

The ritual, spiritual voice of voices is music. This is the voice of
ecstasy, grief, jubilation and praise. In Whitman's ecstatic poetry,
music and song are the metaphors returned to again and again to
encompass the shout of joy that he calls creation:

> O to make the most jubilant song!
> Full of music – full of manhood, womanhood, infancy!
> Full of common employments – full of grain and trees.
>
> O for the voice of animals – O for the swiftness and
>   balance of fishes!
> O for the dropping of raindrops in a song!
> O for the sunshine and motion of waves in a song!
>
> O the joy of my spirit – it is uncaged – it darts like
>   Lightening!
> It is not enough to have this globe or a certain time,
> I will have thousands of globes and all time.[5]

This web of connection between ritual, spirituality and music is at the heart of the exploration bringing together this set of articles. All the contributions have evolved through seminars, performances or personal contact with the Chant and Ritual Song programme at the Irish World Music Centre, University of Limerick, and illustrate the close links that have developed between this programme and worlds as diverse as the Benedictine community at Glenstal Abbey, Limerick; Southern Methodist University, Dallas; the Wilfrid Laurier Department of Religion and Culture, Canada; and the School of Oriental and African Studies, London. As well as a number of significant Irish voices, it includes contributions from scholars, performers and liturgists from the United States, Canada, Croatia, Greece and Zimbabwe.

Ronald Grimes begins the discussion by reminding us that the exploration is of our time: 'spirituality is in vogue'. From its contemporary New Age guise, to the fashionable appropriation of Native American spirituality (paralleling aspects of the current flush of interest in 'Celtic' spirituality) or the politicising of spirituality through feminist or equality interest groups, Grimes traces a subtle and often problematic route through notions of 'spirituality', 'religion' and 'ritual'. Chartwell Dutiro and Rachel Levay chart similar territory in their discussion of music and spirituality in the global marketplace. Drawing on Chartwell's experience as a *mbira* player in Zimbabwe, the article stresses the impossibility of separating music from ritual in the African context and the dangers of their forced separation in the growing market for 'world-music' recordings.

The relationship between music and ritual is further explored by C. Michael Hawn and in my own article. Hawn delves into the implications of musical style and structure for liturgical efficacy. Demonstrating the differences between sequential musical structures (most commonly found in hymn-forms and usually characterised as strophic, textually oriented, and functioning as a commentary on the ritual), and cyclic musical structures (which tend to involve theme and variation or call and response, and to be associated with oral tradition and ritual activity), he concludes by suggesting the ritual value of both musical forms.

My own preoccupation with how we teach and study ritual music stems from both my research interests and my interaction with students on the chant and ritual song programme. If musicology has taught us the value of studying style, structure and composition in music, ethnomusicology has taught us the equal value of studying the context within which music is performed. Behaviour (music) and context (ritual) go hand in hand in the mapping of ritual music. Approaching the world of religious ritual through the academic lens brings in its wake a multitude of ethical and methodological challenges. Through the use of a new multi-disciplinary model, drawing on hermeneutic philosophy, interpretive anthropology, ritual studies, liturgical theology and music performance, I believe that research in ritual music can reveal new understandings of our need to ritualise and the function of music in this unique aspect of human behaviour.

Drawing the discussion closer to home, Seán Ó Duinn and Barra Boydell explore aspects of Irish spirituality and music. Ó Duinn's treatment of early Irish piety illustrates the over-lapping layers of Celtic and Roman spirituality in Ireland as well as revealing some tensions between traditional devotional practices and official liturgical worship. Boydell traces the earliest evidence of music in medieval Irish liturgy and speculates on the tantalising remnants of an earlier liturgical music.

The voice of chant has a long and wide association with religious ritual. Through the medium of personal interviews, Katarina Livljanic and Ioannis Arvanitis share their journeys as performers of Western plainchant and Byzantine music.

The creative impulse in art and spirituality is explored by Mark Patrick Hederman and Mícheál Ó Súilleabháin. Hederman addresses Heidegger's reading of poetry (noting that 'for Heidegger, the notion of "poetry" and "art" are almost interchangeable') as a means through which human consciousness 'reaches beyond the modality of thinking that is philosophical or scientific.' In the creative process, the poet or artist becomes a medium through which truth emerges: a truth unsayable and unknowable through rational discourse. The end of philosophy, or the opening of philosophy to another kind of thinking and expressing, is an opening towards the 'Other'.

Ó Súilleabháin explores this same creative process in the domain of music. Once again, creativity is seen as both the means by which humanity survives and, simultaneously, gives meaning and articulation to that existence: 'as the very essence of things fall away before our every moment, our survival rests upon our ability to invest each living moment with a creativity born of the spirit'. Musical creativity is the imagination and the body 'throwing shapes' into the wind; it is a game of architecture built from sound and, at its most spiritual, it is the 'singing body', the body at prayer.

Where music meets spirituality, theology often follows. Three aspects of this relationship are explored by Cyprian Love, Fintan Lyons and Nóirín Ní Riain. Love notes that, 'for Christian theology, in the whole of created being, there is no such thing as neutrality.' Creation is not static or passive but constantly drawn upwards and inwards towards God. Viewing liturgy as *theologia prima*, a primary source of theology, Love suggests that liturgy manifests this theological longing in the spontaneity of its expression. It follows then that, 'a characteristically liturgical form of music should be evanescent, not like permanent composition, and should share in the liturgical movement of becoming-into-God'. Organ improvisation, such as that expounded by Charles Tournemire, exemplifies this use of music as theology.

Lyons explores a different angle of this relationship, noting the use of music to re-enforce theological positions as well as the influence of theological change on musical expression. Through a review of the role of church music in the Reformation, Lyons traces the recognition of music as a means of promoting theological reform in, for example, Luther's use of German hymns, to the rejection of music exemplified in Zwingli's famous removal of organs from the churches of Geneva.

While both these articles explore the relationship between theology and music, Ní Riain's contribution suggests that music itself may be viewed as a kind of theology, a 'theosony'. Drawing on traditions of mystical revelation and religious experience, music is viewed as a means of experiencing 'insight into the presence of God', as a 'privileged means of encounter'. Similar to Heidegger's view of poetry as a language beyond philosophical or scientific discourse, Ní

Riain suggests that 'theosonance' is 'the religious dimension of human hearing' – the ability to hear beyond 'mundane sound' and to listen in a new way.

The set of articles concludes with two contributions representing the worlds of art, or aesthetics, and science. Often viewed as opposite poles in human understanding, these articles suggest that both aesthetics and science may have something to contribute to concepts of spirituality and healing. Gerard Gillen's article, towards a definition of 'good' liturgical music, grasps the nettle of aesthetics in a courageous and unequivocal manner. The challenge to create ways of knowing, or criteria for evaluating the value and quality of music in ritual, is addressed as central to the efficacy of the ritual itself. Kaja Jensen's article, from the perspective of a music therapist, notes the power of music to move or heal or destroy, giving added urgency to the weight of Gillen's conviction that musical choices, in ritual or in life, have profound implications for the nature of experience. Drawing on conditions as diverse as Alzheimer's and AIDs, Jensen's case studies suggest that music often plays a common role in explanations of scientific and spiritual 'healing'.

This view is echoed and may be illustrated by referring again to Kenzaburo Oe. In 1963, his first son was born with a cerebral hernia and resulting surgery left him permanently brain damaged. Oe describes Hikari as a baby responding only to the chirping of birds and, later, 'being awakened by the voices of birds to the music of Bach and Mozart'.[6] In 1995, a year after receiving the Nobel Prize for Literature, Oe declared that he would not write fiction any more, for Hikari, now a successful composer despite his handicap, no longer needed his father to speak for him.

The Irish World Music Centre is dedicated to performance and research in the performing arts of music and dance. This collection of essays represents a very special aspect of that exploration, probing the role of music as a performative voice in ritual and as an expression of spirituality. The ability of music to articulate beyond the tangible or the rational, to voice humanity's wonder and grief as well as acting as an agent of change and healing, emerges as a motif in several of the contributions. Like religious ritual, music is often the voice and expression of the incomprehensible at the root of existence. Like all forms of spirituality, it attempts the impossible but necessary encounter between creation and creator through the only possible voice recognisable to both: the striving soundings of creativity.

Notes

1. Edmund White, *The Farewell Symphony* (New York: Vintage, 1997), p. 413.
2. Sophocles, *Antigone*, trans. by Richard Emil Braun (Oxford University Press, 1973), p. 39.
3. William Styron, *Lie Down in Darkness* (New York, Vintage International, 1951, 1979), p. 248.
4. See introduction to Kenzaburo Oe's *Nip the buds, shoot the kids* (New York, Grove Press, 1958), p. 14.
5. Walt Whitman, 'A Song of Joys' from *The Complete Poems* (London, Penguin Books, 1975), p. 206.
6. Kenzaburo Oe, op. cit., p. 17.

Ritual and Spirituality

Global Spirituality and Ritual[1]

Ronald L. Grimes

SPIRITUALITY IS IN VOGUE. Usually, the notion is not defined. If one persists though, there are definitions to be discovered, for example: 'Spirituality can be described as a process of transformation and growth, an organic and dynamic part of human development, of both individual and society.'[2] Like most of the tacit definitions, this explicit one is troublesome because of its lack of precision; it could be a definition of, say, evolution. The definition seems to endorse an expansionist ideology that values growth, dynamism, and transformation above all else. It assumes an infinite spiritual frontier rather than limited spiritual space.

Not only is the idea of spirituality fashionable among countercultural New Agers who have now become mainstream, white, middle-class people, but it is also a constitutive notion in at least two other groups, as the phrases 'women's spirituality' and 'Native spirituality' suggest. There is a growing and troubling cultural consensus that holds that, one, the word 'spirituality' indicates something desirable and, two, that this something is definitely not religion. In current parlance there is a growing tendency to distinguish sharply between religion and spirituality. In this division of labour, religion is institutional, traditional, perhaps even moribund, while spirituality is personal, spontaneous and alive. Religion, according to this view, is less desirable, largely because of its institutional tethering. The current notion of spirituality is a way of laying claim to a religiosity supposedly not identified with the establishment, that is, with the Christian mainstream. We are witnessing a conscription of the notion of spirituality that aspires to take it beyond its dualistic Christian assumptions and that aims to make it global, that is to say, atemporal and acultural. Spirituality is undergoing a transformation much like those that engulfed the ideas of mysticism, myth, and shamanism in the mid-twentieth century.

In current rhetoric, spirituality is a meta-religion – sort of religious, sort of not. Ordinary folks do not take out membership in it, and it is a virtue that they do not. Alternatively, those who have transcended ordinary denominational religion are 'into' spirituality, sometimes into shamanism, myth, mysticism, and ritual as well. Meanwhile, scholars debate whether spirituality and its tent-mates are really 'there,' actual phenomena in history and culture, or whether they are mere scholarly constructions, patterns, and motifs scissored from their historical and cultural matrices.

In 'new' spirituality circles ritual is a bone of contention. In one moment it is identified with religion; in the next, with spirituality. Until recently, spirituality and ritual were imagined as opposites: ritual was physical, exterior, superficial and institutional, while spirituality was metaphysical, interior, deep and personal. In both scholarly and popular usage, ritual is still largely religious, collective, repetitive and traditional. For a growing minority though, ritual is becoming a tool of exploration, a means of pursuing personal spirituality, an expression of personal creativity.

In discussions with Native North American scholars and students, it usually creates less trouble to speak of Native 'spirituality' rather than Native 'religion', since religion is regularly identified with organised religion, especially Christianity. It makes little difference that the term 'spirituality' is much more tied to the apron strings of Christianity than the word religion ever was, that the idea of spirituality has a sordid history entangled with asceticism, piety and Western dualism, or that the current generic use is a substantial reversal of that history. Despite the antagonism that Native North American people sometimes show towards New Age appropriation, there is agreement between the two groups that spirituality is desirable, while religion is not. So the issue is not whether one speaks of 'spirituality' or 'religion', but what we mean by each term when we utter or write it. For Native people the important point is that spirituality should not be cordoned off, restricted to some specific sector considered 'religious,' and also that spirituality cannot be learned from texts or taught in classrooms.

Native people are usually less ambivalent about ritual than the New Age crowd is.[3] Native Americans assume spirituality to be inextricably linked to ceremony and community. Spirituality is not understood individualistically, nor is it opposed to ceremonial form. In addition, Native spirituality is not a species of so-called global spirituality but rather is linked to specific places. When non-Native people use the idea of spirituality to refer to a 'religion' that transcends time and space, it continues the legacy of Christianity, which, by considering itself the religion of no particular time and place became, in its own eyes, the religion of all times and places.[4]

In discussions with Native people it is important to recognise not only differences in how 'spirituality' is used but also in how 'ritual' is understood. In anthropological discourse after Victor Turner, 'ritual' has became desirable and 'ceremonial' suspect, since he associated the former with creativity and transformation and the latter with the status quo. These connotations are now being picked up in popular parlance. But in Native discussions, 'ceremony' remains the preferred term, and it usually seems to connote 'sacred ceremony'.

One of the persistent difficulties in discussing spirituality and ritual are the dualisms, the sets of opposition, that persist in the English language, for instance: word/action and body/spirit. Since both of these bedevil the study and practice of ritual, they require attention. Actions and words are sometimes set in opposition: 'Actions speak louder than words.' Where actions and language are made enemies, ritual is usually identified with action and regarded as irrational and emotional, leaving language as the principle of knowledge and rationality. But in actual rites, actions and words are often partners, not enemies. Though they may be dissonant with one another, each is linked inextricably to the other. In ritual settings, myths are told, hymns chanted, creeds recited, testimonies uttered, orations presented, scripture read, and homilies delivered. Some rites are constructed almost exclusively of words. Words are so important to ritual that we in the West sometimes carelessly speak of words as if they were the whole of ritual. We refer to weddings, for example, as the saying or exchanging of vows, thereby ignoring all but the linguistic features of the ceremony.

The body/mind, or body/spirit, split is as dangerous as the action/word dualism. Spiritual people, however, do not escape their bodies. Even when ritual actions induce trance and participants communicate with spirits in so exclusive a way that they forget their own bodies and cannot remember their own deeds, they nevertheless do so as embodied human beings. No matter how disembodied a rite or how preoccupied a theology with things of the head or spirit, bodies do not evaporate. Bodies are required in order to perform their own contempt or rejection.

The new 'global' spirituality is as critical of these various dualisms as I am, so there is no need to labour their critique. But since this newly configured, largely polemical idea of spirituality is making its way into the academy,[5] it is time we paid critical attention to it and examined its uses. For those little interested in the topics, religion, spirituality, and ritual may seem birds of a feather, even synonyms, but surely scholars require more nuanced usage. Robert Torrance's *The Spiritual Quest: Transcendence in Myth, Religion, and Science* is, I believe, the most comprehensive cross-cultural work on contemporary spirituality.[6] Although he exemplifies current trends in defending and advocating spirituality, he attempts to put the concept on a solid scholarly footing and tries to correct some of the popular abuses and misconceptions. His argument that there is a transcultural spirituality is more scholarly than many others, for instance, those articulated by Joseph Campbell and most Jungians. Torrance shares, however, many of the prejudices of pop spirituality (the counterpart of pop psychology). For instance, he takes religion to be 'the hypostatized inertia (or 'repository of sacred tradition') by which society collectively denies the potentially disruptive reality of change.'[7]

Torrance does not formally define spirituality, but he does say that spirit is 'the dynamic potentiality latent but unrealized in the given.'[8] He uses 'spiritual quest' and 'quest' much as others use 'spirituality.' He says quest is 'the deliberate effort to transcend, through self-transformation, the limits of the given and to realize some portion of this unbounded potentiality through pursuit of a future goal that can neither be fully foreknown nor finally attained.'[9] In this way he renders religion and spiritual quest as polarities, with religion playing the role of cultural conservative, while spirituality is cast in the romantic role of bold and future-oriented culture hero. As Torrance's argument develops and its sweep increases, religion is rendered collective, and spiritual quest, individualistic. His book becomes an implicit critique of collective religion.

Torrance construes myth and ritual, spirit possession and shamanism as expressions of spiritual quest. In doing so, he marshals an impressive array of cross-cultural data, introducing readers to a veritable banquet of spiritual morsels imported from the corners of the globe. The problem with such a layout is that each morsel is tiny, a delicacy, and its place on the Western conceptual table is more obvious than its place back on its home table. Though the invitation is never quite explicitly offered, readers seem to be invited to partake. We are repeatedly tempted by descriptions of the excellence of the fare.

Unlike many of the spirituality popularisers, Torrance does not locate its imputed universality in either archetypes and the collective unconscious, or in an assumed perennial philosophy. His claims about universality are usually arguments, not assumptions (typically, the basis of popular discourse about spirituality). The basis of his claim is scientific research that suggests the roots of spiritual questing lie in human biology – even in matter itself. Torrance argues a provocative idea: liminality is implicit in the very operation of the brain itself. He tries to show how 'the ternary process' of van Gennep (the ritual sequence – separation, transition, incorporation) is not just a convenient analytical scheme (which is the view held by most cultural anthropologists) but a description of the inherent nature of reality itself.[10] Ternary relation, he argues, is at the heart of all process; it is the dynamic by which things continually transcend themselves. One has to work hard to resist reading such a claim as specific to the cultural complex that produced the doctrine of the Trinity and the idea of the dialectic of history.

The cross-cultural breadth and interdisciplinary seriousness of Torrance's argument is admirable, but I have strong reservations about it. Torrance generates too many stereotypes that take on the status of theories. Certain notions, religion and ritual, for example, are made to carry the 'bad-guy' load. Ritual, like religion, is defined as essentially closed, invariant, and confirmatory. On this score Torrance sounds more like a mid-century anthropologist than like New Age ritual enthusiasts.

Myth, thinks Torrance, is quite different from ritual. Myth is open and typified by 'creative variability.'[11] Unlike, say, Victor Turner, who found both closed ('status system' or 'structural') and open ('liminal') elements in ritual, Torrance polarises the theoretical constructs. Predictably, one polarity is cast in a better light than the other; there is a hierarchy. This decided preference for the moving, creative, and open is consistent with the Bergsonian philosophy that drives much of Torrance's vision of spirituality. Late in his argument Torrance begins to declare that the polarities, for instance, priestly ritual and shamanistic quest, are not exclusive opposites; rather they are complementary. But the definitional opposition upon which he earlier depended reasserts itself, leaving him unable to see, for instance, the closedness of spirituality and the openness of religion.

I have no objection to treatments of spirituality that argue for its universality or that try to predicate universality on subatomic physics or human biology. I do, however, think such strategies are impoverished if they lack cultural self-awareness, overt recognition of the cultural and historical specificity of their own governing ideas, in this case: spirit, quest, religion, ritual and shamanism. I am reminded of a comment a Native American colleague once made: 'Every time, he said, I hear a white person use the term "spirituality" rather than "religion", I worry, because I know that person is in the process of packaging for export the very practices I grew up with and continue to revere.'

I wish Torrance and others like him wrote with more awareness of the politics of spirituality, with more cunning about ways the idea underwrites the expropriation of other people's beliefs, stories, and practices. I wish advocates of contemporary spirituality recognised how Western their 'universal' spirituality sounds to non-Western ears. If they did, they would say more about the connections among spiritual questing, heroic individualism, and colonial expansionism. Torrance and others are in danger of colluding with all three. I worry about Torrance's evaluative, evolutionary assumptions. He believes the 'fullest realization' of the quest for 'indeterminate transcendence' is to be found in America.[12] We never learn what the criteria are for such an ethnocentric judgement.

For Torrance, the *locus classicus* of spiritual questing is in the Great Plains of North America, which, he says, is largely free of 'priestly inflexibility', and which is a place where shamanism is 'democratized'.[13] What is the effect of 'discovering' the paradigmatic expressions of spiritual questing in the heart of the American midwest? How different is this strategy from envisioning the United States as the New Eden? What difference does it make that now American Plains Indians rather than European-American Christians are the heroes of this 'new' spirituality? Surely, readers must wonder, if not suspect, that such a valuation has more to do with the author's national and cultural values than with the Lakota Sun Dance. I worry that the function (not the intention) of such an argument is to set up Plains practices as a spirituality-for-the-taking. Unlike New Age writers, Torrance does not actually counsel appropriation, but neither does he advise against it. He does not even raise the issue, and he works to make spiritual questing *the* appetising religious alternative.

By his implicit value judgements, Torrance at once privileges certain forms of spiritual questing and endangers them. The native heroes of his spiritual quest are the same as those of New Age spirituality: Nicholas Black Elk, John Fire Lame Deer, Frank Fools Crow. Spirituality in the form of visionary shamanism is, it seems, good religion, ideal religion, paradigmatic religion. Vision quests become in Torrance's writing a cipher encoding the values of contemporary, white American culture: openness to the future, flexibility, lack of priestly hierarchy, strong emphasis on individuality, objectivity, essential unfinishedness, and so on. I believe that Torrance's position – although he would probably deny it – is a religious one and that this book is a tacit theological argument for the superiority of spiritual questing over other, more 'denominational', more 'priestly' forms of religion.

Torrance, like several other contemporary scholars (but unlike his New Age compatriots), operates with a linguistic bias, an assumed rather than demonstrated priority of language (and its usual champion, metaphor). Perhaps he expresses his disciplinary biases in doing so; he teaches comparative literature. Language, he says, is *the* instrument of spiritual questing: 'And unlike the fixed movements of the dance, language, once released by the solvent of trance from the formulaic repetitiveness of ritual, can never be confined to the self-referential closure of communicating absence of newness . . .'[14] Torrance repeatedly assumes or asserts the superiority of language to action, hence the superiority of myth to ritual, even though by the end of the book he is trying to construe them as partners. His vision culminates in what I call 'readerly heroism': Readers of narratives (such as myths or novels) are metaphoric heroes, and heroes are metaphoric vision questers. I do not deny that there are parallels between reading and spiritual questing,[15] but the differences between reading myths or novels and undergoing vision quests on Mount Harney could hardly be more pronounced.

Spiritual questing, Torrance believes, is superior to mere ritual because of questing's apparent consistency with contemporary science, especially quantum mechanics, and with literature, especially the act of reading novels. In Torrance, American romanticism is alive and well. It is as unaware as it has ever been that positive stereotyping entraps just as surely as negative stereotyping does. A de-ritualised, visionary, supposedly global spirituality is a mess of pottage that no one but a Noble Savage could survive on, and there are no such savages on the Great Plains. There never were.

My primary aim has been critical rather than constructive, but we need definitions of religion, spirituality, and ritual that subvert or cross-cut sets of polar opposites, and that are also less universalised and idealised. Imagine, for instance, that we define rites as *sequences of action rendered special by virtue of their condensation, elevation, or stylisation; spirituality as practiced attentiveness aimed at nurturing a sense for the interdependence of all beings sacred and all things ordinary; and religion as spirituality sustained as a tradition or organised into an institution.* Defined this way, religion, spirituality and ritual are not synonymous. But neither is the personal the opposite of the social, the sacred split off from the profane, nor religion and ritual made the enemy of spirituality. I make no claim that these are flawless definitions. My point is only to illustrate one way of trying to differentiate and connect ideas important to the discipline of religious studies. It makes little sense to let spirituality and religion be mere synonyms, but it also makes no sense to set them up as opposites with one superior to the other.

Notes

1. Originally published as 'Forum: American Spirituality', *Religion in American Culture* 9.2 (1999), 145–152.
2. Ursula King, *Women and Spirituality: Voices of Protest & Promise* (London: Macmillan, 1989), p. 5.
3. I am thinking here of several electronic discussions of Native spirituality. The most recent one was on NATIVELIT_L@listproc2.mail.cornell.edu, from 25 March through 5 April 1996. A more sustained one is reported in Ronald L. Grimes, 'This May Be a Feud, But It Is Not a War: An Electronic, Interdisciplinary Discussion of Teaching Native American Religions', *American Indian Quarterly* 20.3 (1996), 433–450.
4. An excellent discussion of this tendency is Tod Swanson, 'To Prepare a Place: Johannine Christianity and the Collapse of Ethnic Territory', *Journal of the American Academy of Religion* 62.2 (1994), 241–263.
5. See, for instance, Sandra M. Schneiders, 'Spirituality in the Academy', *Modern Christian Spirituality*, ed. by Bradley C. Hanson (Atlanta: American Academy of Religion, 1990), p. 23; also her 'Theology and Spirituality: Strangers, Rivals, or Partners?' *Horizons* 13 (1986), 266.
6. Robert M. Torrance. *The Spiritual Quest: Transcendence in Myth, Religion, and Science* (Berkeley: University of California Press, 1994).
7. Ibid., p. 4.
8. Ibid., p. xii.
9. Ibid., p. xii.
10. Ibid., pp. 269, 271.
11. Ibid., p. 95.
12. Ibid., p. 28.
13. Ibid., pp. 248, 294.
14. Ibid., p. 123.
15. In fact, I argue for them in *Reading, Writing, and Ritualising* (Washington, DC: Pastoral Press, 1993).

Voices of Ancestors:
Music and Spirituality in the Global Marketplace

Chartwell Dutiro and Rachel Levay

ALL OVER AFRICA, music takes a central role in spirituality, and not only in terms of its ceremonial function. Like waves rippling from a drop of water in a pool, its influences radiate outwards to have a powerful effect on wider society, both traditional and contemporary.

Music makes its presence felt in various contexts in Zimbabwean Shona culture. People sing while they work, they sing when sad, they sing when they are happy. The most important occasion for playing music is at a *bira* (festival). There are different kinds of *mapira* (festivals): some are ritualistic and others are simply for celebration. In traditional ceremonies the whole community gathers to participate in the ritual. African religion is based predominantly upon participation, rather than upon adherence to ideology. Participation of the whole community is essential to the expression of group spirituality. Music and dance give every person in society a role in the ceremony and encourage joint responsibility and a general sense of unity. The individual musical elements are often essentially simple, and become interlocked with many participants to create a complex whole, through clapping, singing, yodelling and dancing.

Music and dance are crucial for the communication process within spiritual ceremonies, and, as in much African music, are interdependent and not seen as separate elements. Dance provides percussion, with the stamping of the feet often enhanced by shakers attached to the body; it gives physical expression of and a further dimension to the music; it makes firm contact with the sacred space and the earth's energies, and it also provides a strong visual reference. Dancing a certain dance to music that belongs to a particular spirit lets the whole group understand and recognise that spirit. The music played will identify, or call, a spirit, and the dancing will then manifest that spirit to the community, setting up a kind of dialogue with the music of the participants.

In ritualistic performance, professional *mbira* players are highly respected since their music is influential in invoking the spirits of departed kings or ancestors to come and possess the spirit medium. It is the clan spirits of the dead that must be given due respect in most ritual performances, and it is during such performances that the community can speak to the dead. Past heroes and heroines are praised; their past reputation and fame signified by their totem clan animal is honoured. Here, the *mbira* player is a catalyst in spirit possession and the totem clan animal binds the community together as part of their identity.

A good musician will have a very broad repertoire so as to be able to pick exactly the right songs for any spirit that might come. Some *mbira* songs lay stress on issues of national importance, such as petition for rain or for war. The musicians play until the music reaches a certain dimension where it gels with the participants and with the spirits. It is their job to build and maintain a kind of musical platform on which the drama of the ceremony can unfold, and once the proceedings start in earnest, they must not allow the music to deviate from the groove or make any mistakes that might break the magic. As the medium provides a physical body for the spirit to inhabit temporarily, the musicians provide the musical context for the spirits to inhabit.

The musical instruments used in trances involving spirit possession have a very special significance: they are often invested with mystical powers, and can confer power on the players themselves. The onset of trance is a very mystical moment, and the fact that music is credited with inducing this state gives magical properties to the music and the music maker. In Shona *bira* ceremonies, the *mbira*[1] is the foremost instrument and the most beloved by the ancestors. It is revered for its complexity in that it is both a percussive instrument in the plucking thumb movements, a melodic instrument in the tuning of the keys, and an idiophone[2] in the buzzing of the shells or bottle tops. Several different interlocking parts are played together by different musicians, creating polyphonic music with a complex set of rhythms and melodic parts, accompanied by singing, *hosho* shakers, percussion, clapping and dance. Many instruments, including drumming patterns and singing styles, are reflected in the playing of the *mbira*. The *mbira* therefore comes to represent all constituent parts of the music in one, and mbira players are the most highly respected musicians in Shona society. The *mbira* also figures strongly in Shona mythology, as a source of power and magical protection. The fact that the ancestors themselves may play *mbira* also gives players a special link to the spirit world. The best sound of *mbira* at a festival must resound as if it is being played inside water: the sacred pool of Nyamhita.[3]

Mbira players may be chosen at a very young age if it is seen that their playing attracts the spirits quickly and reliably, and players can build up reputations that mark them out for miles around as the best musician to draw the spirits.

> I started to play at the age of four in spiritual ceremonies, often playing through the whole night, and having to get up and go to school, or even, paradoxically, to Sunday school, the next day. I was sometimes paid with a chicken and a pot of traditional beer for the elders to drink. The chicken may lay eggs and from those eggs more chicks may hatch. The chickens may be exchanged for a goat, which may in turn produce young which could be exchanged for cattle. In this way it is possible for *mbira* players to acquire a great deal of wealth in a village.
>
> (Chartwell Dutiro)

The learning of *mbira* is an important process, as it is one of the carriers of the mysteries of the Shona culture, and must be passed on from one generation to the next. In true archetypal style, the most honoured and authentic way of learning *mbira* is to be taught directly by the ancestors in a dream. *Mbira* players, by tradition, are often travelling musicians, and need not necessarily come from the locality, as long as they know all the right songs to please the ancestors. In fact, it is in some ways better that the musicians remain emotionally and spiritually disinterested so that they can fulfil their role without distraction. One of the main reasons why musicians need to be detached is so that they are less likely to become possessed, thereby becoming unable to fulfil their important role as musician.

The social and political power of possession ceremony music did not always go unnoticed by the colonial authorities, and its performance was widely prohibited across Africa. Native instruments were highly suspect because of colonial denominational competition. The *bira* was an obstacle to religious progress, and *rombe*, or musician, began to acquire its contemporary negative connotation of 'vagabond'.[4] Missionaries, for example, banned traditional music in favour of sung hymns in four-part harmony.

> When I was twenty I moved to Harare and joined a brass band, which was government sponsored under the prison service. Here I learned the saxophone and rudiments and theory of music. We were taught to play 'real' music. For the eight years I was there I didn't play *mbira* at all.
>
> (Chartwell Dutiro)

Music from spirit possession ceremonies also has its influence in secular settings by becoming absorbed into other popular types of music. This is particularly true since the rise of African nationalism and a rekindled respect for traditional music. In *Chimurenga* music in Zimbabwe, for example, which was born out of the Zimbabwean liberation struggle, the sound of *mbira* was transferred to guitar, and traditional drums were replaced with drumkits in order to appeal to the new urbanised generation. Along with lyrics of dissent and political uprising by musicians such as Thomas Mapfumo during the war of independence, the musical heritage gives contemporary music a huge depth, strength and sense of cultural history. However, the stigma of the itinerant traditional musician remained.

> I joined Thomas Mapfumo and the Blacks Unlimited in 1986, playing *mbira* and saxophone. The band had previously had no *mbira* in the line-up, and had simply reproduced the sound in

a damping strings technique known as *mbira* style guitar. Despite the desire to include the traditional *mbira* in the group, I was considered to be slightly less of a 'real' musician than the others, and was paid accordingly.

(Chartwell Dutiro)

Mbira music has never been passed down through written musical notation, but rather from generation to generation through oral memory and sometimes through dreams. In this sense, most *mbira* arrangements are considered traditional, and in copyright law are in the public domain. This means that any *mbira* song used for recording purposes does not even mention the traditional origin of the song and its lyrical style. The new song is taken to be the original and the band leader takes copyright of the 'new' song. Sometimes even the band leader is ignorant about what copyright is, never mind what royalties he is entitled to. In this case, the rights of composition and copyright are often handed over to the record company, so that both the *mbira* player and the band leader lose all rights.

In terms of musicians rights, I don't know of many African musicians who are members of the Musicians Union, although I am one. There is very little that the Performing Rights Society are doing for African Musicians, although they are supposed to be responsible for collecting all the money for music played on radio, TV, etc. The money rarely reaches the musicians.

(Chartwell Dutiro)

This is one of the many problems that plague the transition of traditional music into the global marketplace. There is a long history of marketing 'exotic' music from far away places, from the Great Exhibitions of the late 1800s, which included musical curiosities from all over the world, to the present day promoting of 'world music'. Globalisation has engendered a greater interest in other cultures, and a growing sense of the need to understand these cultures as we all slowly get to grips with the fact that we are all interdependent and increasingly culturally intertwined.

The term 'world music' was coined in 1987 at a meeting of independent record labels, music journalists and promoters, whose main objective was simply to find a way of marketing music from around the world to the British public – literally, what should be written on the box in the record shop. Many of the individuals at that meeting have gone on to become mainstays of the 'world music' industry, which has flourished under their direction, opening people's hearts and minds to the music of the world.

However, voices are now being raised against this homogenous term, 'world music'. Firstly, public consciousness around music from different cultures is much more developed than it was ten or fifteen years ago, and the music itself has diversified hugely through contemporary musical developments throughout the world. Even what we see as traditional music can only ever be seen as music within a tradition, rather than as a static phenomenon. It is no longer acceptable for both practical and ethical reasons for all music that isn't Western to be lumped together in this random way. It sets up a false boundary between 'us' and 'them'; it exoticises the music from other cultures, and it entrenches the idea that Western music is the norm. This is particularly difficult to relate to when Western culture itself is now so ethnically mixed.

One of the problems that traditional music faces in the 'world music' arena is that it is most often performed and listened to out of context. The very process of recording traditional music and playing it back on radio or CD produces a false experience of the music. It is what Kurt Blaukopf calls 'secondary aurality'.[5] Traditional music does not always record well. It may be repetitious by nature, designed to be performed over several hours. It may be intrinsically linked with dance, which must necessarily be omitted from the exclusively aural experience of a sound recording, and the music often has to be changed somewhat in order to be understood 100 per cent aurally. Essentially, participatory music is consumed passively, so that only a fraction of its essential experience is transmitted. Or the music may be relevant to a certain cultural context, which cannot be reproduced in a recording. In order to make this music accessible to the 'world music' market, western producers and artists are often brought on board to create a sound more palatable to western ears. In the case of *mbiras*, for example, there is often conflict between a musician and a producer who wants to the strip away the buzzing effect, as it might sound like a speaker malfunction.

> On a number of occasions I was told while recording that 'we are going to put gaffa tape around your shells and bottle tops to stop the buzzing'. I was asked to listen to the resulting *mbira* sample, which sounded as clear as a glockenspiel. I also once worked with a house music producer on his CD. He wanted to keep the songs to six minutes long, insisting that we had to think about what would sell rather than about the traditional repertoire. These producers now design the sound of the *mbira;* the spirit of the *mbira* is lost and the player also loses the feeling for the music.
>
> (Chartwell Dutiro)

In the live context, this inappropriateness in the presentation of music can be very evident. Many international artists enjoy touring the world and playing to different audiences. However, taking traditional artists from around the world and setting them down in an unfamiliar setting, completely out of context, can produce a very uncomfortable spectacle. Traditional music is often linked to a specific social activity within which it makes total sense, but outside of which it can lose some of its coherence. This is particularly true of religious or ceremonial music, which can seem quite anomalous outside of its natural setting. For example, *mbira* music is designed to be performed through the night to a highly engaged and participating audience, not in an hour's slot in the afternoon at a 'world music' festival. Peddling traditional artists up and down the country on national tours can be an exhausting and unrewarding experience for the artist, both financially and culturally. When there is a CD to market, live music becomes a promotional tool, rather than the foremost goal or the principle experience of the music. Paradoxically, record companies can go to great lengths to reproduce this live sound on CD. It is really positive that audiences are opening their ears to music from around the world, but it is time to re-assess the 'world music' industry both in terms of recordings and live music promotion.

Music is sometimes given the distinction of being a universal language, but in reality it isn't – especially when we do not even understand the lyrics. We can appreciate other people's music to a certain degree, and it can certainly open up our minds to other cultures, but to really understand what informs that music we really need to search deeper and to educate ourselves. Music is part of a cultural ecosystem, as Peter Baumann[6] puts it, and to really understand music we need to understand the wider cultural context.

> As a musician I believe that music can heal the heart and build bridges between cultures. I can do my best to communicate this spirituality through *mbira* music, but a bridge has to be built from both sides, and we need to trust each other. To really open your hearts to the music you need to be totally involved, mind, body and spirit.
>
> (Chartwell Dutiro)

Notes

1. The *mbira* is a lamelophone, consisting of a set of metal keys that are plucked by the thumbs and fingers, and which are attached to a sound board, itself placed inside a resonator or gourd. Bottle tops or shells are attached to the gourd to produce a distinctive buzzing sound. There are several different types of *mbira* in Zimbabwe and surrounding countries.
2. An idiophone is a self-sounding instrument, which does not require a membrane, vibrating strings or breath/air.
3. Nyamhita is a famous heroine who drowned in a pool, which is still held sacred.
4. Originally *rombe* was a Shona word that referred to a travelling medicine man. The term was transferred to musicians because of their similarly itinerant lifestyle.
5. Peter Max Bauman (ed.) *World Music – Musics of the World.* See article by Kurt Blaukopf, 'Mediamorphosis and Secondary Orality: A Challenge to Cultural Policy' (Wilhemlmshaven: Florian Noetzel, 1992).
6. Ibid.

MUSIC AND RITUAL

Form and Ritual: A Comparison between Sequential and Cyclic Musical Structures and their use in Liturgy

C. Michael Hawn

THE PURPOSE OF THIS ARTICLE is to distinguish between the role of congregational musical styles and musical structures within liturgy. Understanding the relationship between musical structure and the rites and rituals of faith communities may assist musical presiders in understanding their task more thoroughly. Both style and structure have their role in helping congregations participate fully in worship. It has been my experience, however, that practical decisions about the choice of congregational music in liturgy are made primarily on the basis of accessibility of musical style and appropriateness of text. The role of a congregational song's musical structure and how it may inform liturgy is less likely to be taken into consideration. Musical form is a significant factor in determining the effectiveness of the congregation's involvement in the ritual. As a way of exploring the role of musical structures in shaping ritual behaviour, I will focus on the fundamental characteristics and ritual uses of sequential and cyclic musical structures with reference to hybrid forms derived from these.

Characteristics of sequential musical structures

As is the case with many Protestants, I was nurtured in worship through the singing of hymns. By hymns I am referring to metered poetry set in several stanzas. The sequential structure of classic Western hymnody is evident in the development of a theological theme over several stanzas. A basic theological concept or scriptural pericope comes to light in stanza one. Stanza two develops this theme or continues the scriptural paraphrase, and so on, until the hymn climaxes in a concluding stanza that draws all of the points together into a whole. The climax of the hymn may be strengthened by a doxological formula, an eschatological reference, a cosmic allusion, or a strong hermeneutical application. A hymn tune sustains the sequential progression of the poetry by being recycled for each stanza. Skilful organists add musical variety by phrasing according to the text of each stanza, providing dynamic contrast, and varying articulation according to the development of the text. An exceptional organist might modify the harmonies discreetly from stanza to stanza in hope of furnishing the text with a more interesting musical foundation.

Organists, hoping to realise both poetic and musical climax, may employ a variety of musical strategies, especially on the final stanza. These could include an increased fullness in organ registration, the use of an alternate harmonisation (implying that the congregation should sing in unison), or a change in tonal centre, usually ascending through a modulation following the penultimate stanza to a key a semitone higher than the previous stanzas.

Given the sequential nature of the text, its teleological character is inherent: a classic western hymn text is going somewhere. One must note where the text begins and follow carefully the progression of thought through to its conclusion, a process that may be done in as few as three stanzas or as many as seven, eight or more in some of the classic ballad hymns. A strophic musical structure, repeating in its entirety with each stanza, belies the inherently sequential nature of the text. How does the singer know when the text has reached a climax? In addition to following the content of the text carefully, the singer can see the end of the hymn coming on the printed page, e.g., only two stanzas to go. As a literary structure, the singer should encounter an ultimate thought beyond which any further material would be anticlimactic. For example, consider the final stanza of Isaac Watts' famous hymn, 'When I Survey the Wondrous Cross':

> Were the whole Realm of Nature mine,
> That were a Present far too small;
> Love so amazing, so divine,
> Demands my Soul, my Life, my All.[1]

In previous stanzas, the singer has been led through the agony of the crucifixion to a cosmic understanding of what Christ's sacrifice means. There is nothing more that can be said.

Charles Wesley often used an eschatological reference at the culmination of a text.[2] Such is the case in his well-known 'Love Divine, All Loves Excelling':

> Finish then thy new creation,
> Pure and spotless let us be;
> Let us see thy great salvation
> Perfectly restored in thee;
> Changed from glory into glory,
> Till in heaven we take our place,
> Till we cast our crowns before thee,
> Lost in wonder, love and praise.[3]

If one is truly 'lost in wonder, love and praise' in heaven, then there are no further stanzas to sing.

A reference to the triune God is a classic way to bring a hymn to its conclusion. This may be seen as an extension of the practice of Christianising the psalms by adding a *Gloria Patri* at the conclusion of the psalm. Edward Plumptre applies this formula to the concluding stanza of his processional hymn, 'Rejoice, Ye Pure in Heart':

> Then on, ye pure in heart!
> Rejoice, give thanks, and sing;
> Your festal banner wave on high.
> The Cross of Christ your King.
> Praise him who reigns on high,
> The Lord, whom we adore,
> The Father, Son, and Holy Ghost,
> One God for evermore.[4]

Over the centuries, a doxological formula expressing the triune God has become a resting place for prayer, sung or spoken.

The skilled poet employs many other literary techniques to achieve a sense of climax and conclusion in strophic hymnody. As there are too many possibilities to list here, one final approach must suffice. In addition to those given above, a way of concluding a sequentially structured hymn text is to end with a petition. Concluding petitions, found throughout the history of Christian song, call to mind the inherent relationship between singing and praying. This is a relationship that is organically connected to the roots of the Judeo-Christian heritage, though not, of course, limited to Christian tradition.[5] Latin verse often ends with a doxological confession. But, consider briefly the classic petitions found at the conclusion of many Latin poems. These examples, taken from the sequences approved during the Council of Trent, have served as models for hymnic petitions for many centuries since their conception.

From the final stanza of the 'Veni sancte Spiritus' (attr. to Stephen Langton, d. 1228), sometimes called the golden sequence, the imperative form of the Latin verb *dare* (to give or grant) begins four of the final six lines. The metrical translation by John Mason Neale (1852), though indicating three petitions (see italics), obscures the incessant power of the Latin imperative 'da.'

Da tuis fidelibus	*Fill* thy faithful, who confide
in te confidentibus	in thy power to guard and guide
sacrum sepentarium;	with thy sevenfold mystery:
da virtutis meritum;	here thy grace and virtue *send;*
da salutis exitum,	*grant* salvation to the end,
da perenne gaudium.	and in heaven felicity.[6]

The 'Dies Irae' (attr. Thomas of Celano, fl. 1215), concludes with an implied kyrie eleison and the familiar *dona eis requiem.* The metrical translation is by W.J. Irons (1848) as found in the *English Hymnal* (1906):

Lacrymosa dies illa,	Ah! that day of tears and mourning!
quae resurget ex favilla	from the dust of earth returning
iudicandum homo reus,	man for judgement must prepare him;

huis ergo *parce* deus.	*spare*, O God, in mercy *spare* him!
Pie Jesu Domine,	Lord, all-pitying, Jesu blest,
dona eis requiem.	*grant* them thine eternal rest.[7]

In both cases, the petitions are of such gravity that the hymn must end and wait in eschatological hope for a response.

Sequential structures are inherently literary in form. Unless they have a refrain or are sung repeatedly so that they are committed to memory, these forms depend upon the eye for participation. Poetic devices in the Euro-North American cultural context, having evolved over the centuries from Greek and Latin poetry, are often dependant upon visual media.[8] This literary quality has many benefits for ritual. Songs suitable for a given liturgical tradition may be gathered into a single collection. Collections may be organised around the performance of the liturgy and specific rites that constitute a valid enactment of the rituals central to that liturgy. Many collections may have a domestic as well as a corporate life, deepening the personal piety of the participant, and enabling a more complete corporate involvement.[9] While the Roman Catholic tradition also had service books that supported its rites such as the *Liber Usualis* and the Sacramentary, the complexity of these books limited their use only to highly trained and literate professional musicians and clergy. The people did not sing from them so they had no domestic use. Though the Book of Hours was available for private devotions, it was not a formal part of the Mass.[10] Since Vatican II, an array of hymnals have become one option for facilitating the rituals of Catholic liturgy.[11]

Sequential structures use many words. Although recent hymn writers vary classic patterns somewhat, it has proven most effective to organise the many words into stanzas that use a metrical structure and a rhyme scheme. Though guided by the eye on the page, meter and rhyme provide sonorous organisational patterns that aid memory and allow for more cohesive corporate participation. While mnemonic devices are helpful, sequential written forms lend themselves to analysis and a copious use of words.[12] Because of the visual dimension, the singer is clearly aware of the beginning and may anticipate the conclusion of the hymn by seeing how many stanzas remain. The energy comes as both the written text and musical leadership combine to guide the singer toward the climax or culmination of the hymn. In this sense, it is a relatively closed structure – more or less predictable in length and quality of experience – not likely to be open to significant textual or musical variation or improvisation. Furthermore, both the music and the text, as contained on the page, may be kept and reread for further reflection or analysis following the singing of the hymn.

Characteristics of cyclic musical structures

It was during my first visit to the Taizé Community in southeastern France that I became aware of the power of cyclic forms.[13] The music that facilitated the corporate prayer used a very different structure to the hymns of my tradition. The brief texts were sustained by concise musical statements – ostinato, canon, litany, refrain or response. At first the repetitions seemed like sheer redundancy; but after a time I sensed that repetition was not an accurate description of this musical experience. While on the surface, those gathered for corporate prayer might seem to be repeating the same musical mantra over and over again, I discerned that theme and variation was a more apt description of the musical and liturgical experience. A brief song, usually eight to twelve measures in length, consisted of a short theme that shaped one cycle. Each time the theme returned, there were variations: a worshipper might become gradually aware of a deeper centring or relaxation of the body after several cycles; a cantor might sing different scriptural or devotional texts above the primary theme on successive cycles; an instrument might provide a variation on the theme; the singer/prayer might focus on an icon, or hum or sing harmony or become aware of another's harmony. Rather than redundancy, the experience was replete with variation as the main theme returned again and again.

My experience with this form of theme and variation broadened during research and teaching in Africa. Once again, I participated in shorter musical forms with less textual content but in musical styles radically different than the generally meditative sung prayers of Taizé. Though repetition was involved, there were also significant modifications: the leader(s) varied the text in a call-response manner; percussion instruments provided subtle variations; dancers interacted with the percussion and singing; the intensity seemed to gather with each recurrence of the theme. It was not until I spent some time with ethnomusicologist Andrew Tracey in South Africa that I began to understand the broader implications of what he called cyclic musical structures.[14]

Cyclic musical structures embraces a variety of musical styles.[15] Regardless of style, the effective presentation of a cyclic structure or the performance of a ritual in liturgy depends upon establishing a clear distinction between what Ronald Grimes calls boredom and monotony. 'Liturgy as a form of work does not surprise, though it may keep us open to serendipitous moment by its very monotony. . . . Liturgy is a full emptiness, a monotony without boredom, a reverent waiting without expectation.'[16] Tom F. Driver clarifies this idea with his concept of 'ritual boredom' in which rituals 'have lost touch with the actualities of people's lives and are thus simply arcane; or else the people have lost the ability to apprehend their very need of ritual, do not see what rituals are good for, and thus do not find them even potentially valuable.'[17] While popular usage equates 'boredom' with 'monotony,' in this context, a monotonous activity, though repetitive, establishes the safe environment in which a ritual may take place or be performed. By virtue of its repetitive, monotonous character, a ritual may enable the individual to move freely, both cognitively and kinesthetically, within the rule of this safe environment, even to improvise. Monotony has a character of what Driver calls 'ritual performance'. He indicates that all ritual performances

> require limits. . . . This delineation of what to do and not to do is rooted in ritualization's being, . . . a process of channeling and marking, of making pathways for behavior. In order to achieve definite form, ritualization encourages certain acts, *reinforcing them with repetition and slight variation,* while ruling others out. In short, ritual performance requires (and makes) rules of the game, *whether these be known from previous usage or come to be elaborated on the spot.*[18]

Thus, while ritual boredom causes lack of interest and participation, monotony facilitates freedom and safe space, i.e., ritual performance.

Cyclic structures offer a repetitive ground over which numerous variations may take place. Without these variations, the repetition is subject to boredom. Skilfully performed musical variations provide enough difference to avoid boredom, but not so much difference to disturb the benefits of monotony.

Other characteristics of cyclic musical structure include this form's essentially oral/aural nature and the effects that this has on kinesthetic response. Books are not necessary for the performance of cyclic structures in the same way that they facilitate sequential musical forms. In fact, books may impede the embodiment of cyclic song. Songs either may be learned orally or, in the case of Taizé chants, may be acquired initially from a score, which is set aside once the short cycle has been internalised. In the case of African music, movement is essential to the performance of the song. Meditative cyclic structures such as Taizé chants also have a kinesthetic dimension as the singer assumes more comfortable postures that encourage centring. Since closing one's eyes or focusing on an icon would be traditional ways of praying in this manner, achieving a centred state of being may make the use of a book prohibitive. Regardless of mood, cyclic structures encourage a physical response, either toward the ecstatic or toward the meditative, and the use of books ultimately hampers the successful performance of these songs.[19]

Walter Ong is particularly helpful in understanding the characteristics of oral transmission. In comparison to sequential, literate structures that are more analytical, oral transmission is aggregative, i.e., uses parallel terms, phrases, clauses, epithets, and other repetitive devices essential to oral transmission. These phrases often come across as clichés in written discourse.[20] While the literate tradition displays a more copious use of words, oral tradition is more redundant.[21] The communal implications of orality are many. In discussing the 'conservative or traditionalist' nature of orality, Ong notes that 'in a primary oral culture conceptualised knowledge that is not repeated aloud soon vanishes . . . oral societies must invest great energy in saying over and over again what has been learned through the ages.'[22] Furthermore, cyclic structures, unlike sequential ones, are elastic and may easily be extended at will to fit the situation at hand, depending upon the effectiveness of the leader. It is no wonder that cyclic structure and its variants – refrain and responsorial forms – are more common in primarily oral cultures.

Another feature of oral transmission is its improvisatory nature, a characteristic that brings oral tradition, in Ong's terms, 'close to the human lifeworld' of the singers and hearers.[23] A printed text must be general enough to fit a variety of situations, while oral transmission makes it possible to particularise the song for those that are physically present or draw upon experiences shared by a specific group of people. Cyclic structure allows for improvisation by providing a repetitive ground over which contextual elements may be added according to the situation and skill of the lead singer(s). The improvisatory quality of cyclic structures renders the experience more ephemeral and less subject to analysis than the sequential alternative.

Musical anthropologist John Blacking brings together our discussion of cyclic structure and the value of monotony in ritual. He suggests that 'by releasing the brain from the task of immediate attention to environmental stimuli, [music] stimulates creative thinking by allowing the 'memory surface' of the brain to deal with information for its own sake.'[24] Furthermore, 'music itself may generate experiences and thoughts that transcend the extra-musical features of the situation.'[25] It is perhaps at this point that the mantra-like ostinati of the Taizé Community place the singer in a state that allows 'creative thinking' or, in this case, prayer to emerge. Through the unity of prayer and song, one is freed from the teleological imperative that dominates much of the western perspective and engages in a more timeless experience that transcends the empirical realities of the situation. An introduction to the United States edition of Taizé music states that the songs 'express a basic reality of faith that can quickly be grasped by the intellect, and that gradually penetrates the heart and the whole being.'[26] I believe that Ong, Grimes, Driver, Blacking and the Taizé prayer are tied together by a single thread. Music with a cyclic structure most often draws upon orality more than literacy, and a sense of monotony, ritual performance, creative thinking and centred prayer.

Musical structures and ritual

The crux of the matter is not only in choosing among accessible musical styles, but finding the most appropriate musical structure that offers support to particular rites and rituals in a given faith community. Consider for a moment a spectrum of congregational musical forms for use with ritual that includes, on one end, a sequential structure that makes primary use of literate traditions with a focus on textual content. At the opposite end of the spectrum is a cyclic structure that is inherently oral/aural (though text and/or music may be written down at times) and focuses on the shaping of community rather than the communication of content.

There are some caveats to such an approach. First, this model proposes a spectrum of possible musical structures rather than a dichotomy between two distinct poles of musical experience. This indicates that one chooses both sequential and cyclic structures for most liturgies rather than either one or the other.[27] While I have associated building community primarily as a function of cyclic forms, sequential musical structures may also bind an assembly together, especially through increased familiarity. Likewise, cyclic structures always have content, even if they usually use fewer words and more repetitive oral/aural devices. In specific faith traditions a sequential hymn may, through extensive use, become so familiar that it assumes a cyclic status. In this situation, most participants would not need to use books and would be freer to look up and enjoy a visual as well as aural sense of the gathered community.

As in any spectrum there are countless variations between the two poles. For example, refrain forms combine aspects of both sequential and cyclic structures. The stanzas of a hymn with a refrain carry on the sequential characteristics of the form while the refrain itself functions in a cyclic manner. It is no accident that Roman Catholics focused on refrain and responsorial structures in their efforts to establish congregational singing after the reforms of the Second Vatican Council. Responsorial psalmody blends the structures by chanting the psalm text in its entirety on the one hand, and by either interspersing the text with an antiphon from time to time or concluding with a *Gloria Patri* on the other. For those who chant psalms regularly, they experience the long-standing tradition of singing a concluding doxology as a refrain. A sung litany provides another responsorial form that falls in between the sequential/cyclic perspectives on the proposed spectrum. Sung responses such as 'Kyrie eleison,' 'Lord, hear our prayer,' or 'Thanks be to God' that are interlined between appropriate petitions or expressions of thanksgiving add a lyrical quality to the prayers that cannot be achieved by speaking alone. While litanies with brief responses may be written, they may be performed in an aural/oral manner that contributes a fuller sense of praying for the world in the midst of the community rather than offering individual intercessions and petitions.

The liturgical link between sequential and cyclic musical structures is the prayerful quality of the sung word. By prayerful quality, I am not referring to Albrecht Dürer's 'praying hands'. This early sixteenth-century image suggests a private devotional approach to prayer rather than the prayers of the gathered corporate community. Dürer's print has become an icon for the act of praying that has obscured for many the differences between private and public prayer. Paul Bradshaw notes that much that passes as common or cathedral prayer in corporate worship is actually individual or monastic prayer. The intercessions of common prayer

> . . . should be focused not primarily upon ourselves and our own needs, nor even merely on those of other Christians but rather upon the needs of the whole world for which Christ died and which he desires to be saved. . . .
>
> Instead of this global vision of their vocation, Christians easily lapse into prayer that concentrates upon themselves and those near and dear to them.[28]

The incorporation of music as a vehicle for prayer adds several dimensions to the ritual experience. Singing unifies the body as those gathered integrate their voices and bodies in unified rhythms, melodies and harmonies. Singing a prayer adds an element of intentionality to the rite over speaking. By intentionality I mean that the act of singing takes more physical effort than speaking. Furthermore, singing together requires an intentional awareness of the gathered body more than does speaking.[29] Singing also adds diversity to the soundscape of the liturgical experience. Sung responses may come from various communities in the history of the church or places around the world. The culturally specific quality of various musical styles links the prayers of an individual community to worshippers of every place and time. Singing also increases the emotional range of prayer. Rather than being limited to comfortable and predictable emotional responses, the affective aspects of prayer may range from the subtlety of centred prayer in all its serenity to more ecstatic dimensions of fully embodied prayer sustained by singing and dancing. The affective power of sung prayer has been addressed by Don Saliers, who states the following:

> At the heart of our vocation as church musicians and liturgical leaders is the question of how we enable the Church to 'pray well' – to sing and dance faithfully and with integrity. . . . When we are engaged in sung prayer, we are not simply dressing out words in sound; rather, we are engaged in forming and expressing those emotions which constitute the very Christian life itself.[30]

Thus, the prayerful quality of singing, regardless of musical structure, has an ethical dimension. Singing has the power to change faith communities. As Miriam Therese Winter states, 'Who we are is how we pray, and how we pray is who we are becoming. . . . This is essentially why we sing: to express who we are and are becoming.'[31]

In conclusion, I will suggest some basic ways that sequential and cyclic musical structures may interact with specific parts of a rite in order to effectively enhance the congregation's participation. In general, I propose two principles for choosing between sequential or cyclic musical structures. Sequential musical structures work better when sung following a ritual action. Employing the long-established educational prescript of mystagogical catechesis – doing should precede explaining[32] – it follows that the significance of ritual actions, e.g., procession of the Word, sacramental actions, etc., are cemented with a sequential hymn following the action. Sequential hymns offer a lyrical theological explanation for what has been observed and experienced by those assembled. *In general, sequential structures forge unity in the community through singing a common understanding of a ritual following a ritual action.*

In contrast, cyclic musical structures unite organically with ritual actions themselves as they are taking place. One practical reason for this is the fact that the assembly is not as dependent upon holding books or reading texts when participating in cyclic structures. Worshippers may observe and enter in through singing and, when appropriate, dancing as the ritual itself transpires. For example, in many faith communities it is the practice while receiving the Eucharist to move forward toward stations or a communion rail to accept the bread and wine. Singing by the community enhances this ritual action in many ways. However, it has been my experience that singing lesser known sequential hymns frustrates those assembled in that they must hold books in their hands, if they are to sing effectively. Without the use of books, the quality of the singing diminishes considerably. Furthermore, taking a book forward inhibits the reception of the communion elements. What does one do with a hymnbook or order of worship while taking communion? The singing generally is less effective since a high percentage of those participating cannot sing as they move forward. Perhaps even more important to the experience is that a congregation, when singing a less familiar sequential form during a ritual action, may be denied the benefits of becoming more fully aware of both aural and visual representations of community. *In general, cyclic structures forge unity in the community by embodying the ritual itself through singing, praying and moving together.*

Cyclic structures allow all present the opportunity to participate more wholly through singing, whether in the pews or moving forward. Since cyclic songs are primarily transmitted through oral means (even if initially read from a page as an aid to memory), the assembly may look up and sense their participation in the complete ritual. Specific styles of music drawn from other cultures (both historical and contemporary) remind the community that the Lord's Supper is set at a table that transcends all times and places. Cyclic musical structures emphasise the corporate nature of this ritual rather than individual piety. The oral character and kinesthetic potential inherent in cyclic music has a quality of *valency* – that is the quality to unite, interact, react, or merge with other aspects of the environment. It is perhaps this quality that prompted the following statement on sacred music in the *Constitution on Sacred Liturgy:*

> The musical tradition of the universal Church is a treasure of inestimable value, greater even than that of any of other art. The main reason for this preeminence is that, as sacred song closely bound to the text, it forms a necessary or integral part of the solemn liturgy.[33]

It is the quality of valency that allows those assembled to be, in the language of the Second Vatican Council, 'full, conscious and active' participants in the drama suggested by the ritual rather than observers.

In summary, a focus on musical styles rather than structures disguises the underlying function and foundation that congregational singing provides within liturgy. Musical style at its best is an aural representation of how people in varying places and times have responded to the established texts (biblical and traditional) and cultural circumstances of their congregations. Variations in musical style remind us of the myriad ways that the incarnation has been made manifest among us and of the diversity through which the Holy Spirit moves throughout the church. Congregational musical structures, however, may be embodied in a wide range of musical styles. An appropriate use of musical structures speaks to the inherent quality of valency in liturgy – how music relates organically to the established rites and rituals of the faith community.

Notes

1.   Selma L. Bishop, *Isaac Watts: Hymns and Spiritual Songs 1707–1748* (London: The Faith Press, 1962), p. 353.
2.   The eschatological character of Charles Wesley texts has recently been highlighted in Teresa Berger, *Theology in Hymns?*, trans. by Timothy E. Kimbrough (Nashville: Kingswood Books, [1989] 1995), 137ff.

3.   'A Collection of Hymns for the Use of the People Called Methodists', *The Works of John Wesley*, ed. by Franz Hildebrandt and Oliver Beckerlegge (Nashville: Abingdon Press, 1983), VII, p. 547.

4.   *Hymns Ancient and Modern Revised* (Hymns Ancient and Modern, Ltd, 1972), p. 875.

5.   The Jewish heritage of prayer stresses the unity of prayer and song. Music in the early synagogue functioned in three ways according to Eliyahu Schleifer: 'psalmody, cantillation of Scripture, and the liturgical chant in which the statutory prayers were recited by a local worship leader . . .' See Eliyahu Schleifer, 'From Bible to Hasidism', *Sacred Sound and Social Change: Liturgical Music in Jewish and Christian Experience*, ed. by Lawrence A. Hoffman and Janet R. Walton (Notre Dame: University of Notre Dame Press, 1992), p. 24. Although Christianity has its musical roots in this Jewish ethos, evidence suggests that early Christians developed new songs and forms for their embryonic worship. Unlike much of our worship today, Edward Foley suggests that 'there was . . . no sharp distinction between the sung and the spoken, no clear division between what we might call the musical and the non-musical, nor any denial of the fundamental lyricism of Christian worship.' See Edward Foley, *Foundations of Christian Music: The Music of Pre-Constantinian Christianity* (Washington DC: The Pastoral Press, 1992), p. 84. Liturgical scholar Paul Bradshaw states that 'It is often . . . difficult to determine when the New Testament authors are citing topical prayer-forms with which they are familiar and when they are not, *or even to separate hymns from prayers, since both may employ a similar construction.*' Italics mine. See Paul Bradshaw, *The Search for the Origins of Christian Worship* (New York: Oxford University Press, 1992), p. 43.

6.   From Erik Routley, *A Panorama of Christian Hymnody* (Collegeville: The Liturgical Press, 1979), p. 65.

7.   Ibid. Routley notes that the English versification is at best a noble attempt that allows the singer the opportunity to sing the gist of the text with the original melody. His literal translation is as follows: Oh, what a day of tears and lamentation, when man, waiting for judgement, rises from earth's ashes: spare him in that day! Kind Lord Jesus, give them rest! (p. 66)

8.   For a brief reference tool of poetic devices, see Austin C. Lovelance, *The Anatomy of Hymnody* (Chicago: GIA Publications, Inc., 1965), pp. 91–102. For a much more extensive understanding of the literate hymn tradition, see J.R. Watson, *The English Hymn: A Critical and Historical Study* (Oxford: Clarendon Press, 1997).

9.   Among Protestants, inexpensive collections by eighteenth-century hymn writers like Isaac Watts and Charles and John Wesley set the trend in this regard. The Wesleys were particularly concerned that their collections

were affordable to the poor. Since these collections were individually owned, they were used at the Society meetings in corporate contexts and in domestic settings as well. These brief collections were theologically or seasonally organised. See the following facsimile reprints by the Charles Wesley Society: *Hymns on the Lord's Supper* (Bristol, 1745); *Hymns for Our Lord's Resurrection* (London, 1746); *Hymns for Ascension-Day and Hymns for Whitsunday* (Bristol, 1746); *Hymns for the Nativity of Our Lord* (London, 1745).

The *Book of Common Prayer* serves a dual domestic/corporate use for many Anglicans as well. Many faithful Anglicans bring their own copy to worship and refer only minimally to it because of the intimate familiarity with the book. In the Reformed tradition, John D. Witvliet notes the rolls of the Genevan Psalter in shaping both domestic and corporate spirituality. See 'The Spirituality of the Psalter: Metrical Psalms in Liturgy and Life in Calvin's Geneva', *Calvin Theological Journal* 32:2 (November 1997), pp. 273–297, for a thorough explanation of the dynamic of the Genevan Psalter between home and church.

10.   For more detailed information on pre-Vatican II rites and music, see John Harper, *The Forms and Orders of Western Liturgy from the Tenth to the Eighteenth Century* (Oxford: Clarendon Press, 1991).

11.   Other options include seasonal missalettes that usually remain at the church and are not used at home. Recent Catholic hymnals in the United States range from *Worship*, 3rd edn. (GIA, 1986) and *Gather* (GIA, 1988) for traditional Anglo congregations, to *Lead Me Guide Me* (GIA, 1987) for African-American congregations, and *Flor y Canto* (Oregon Catholic Press, 1989) for Spanish-speaking congregations. *Hymnal for the Hours* (GIA, 1989) is for use with daily offices, and *By Flowing Waters* (Liturgical Press, 1999) uses only plainsong style for the liturgy. *Ritual Song* (GIA, 1996) combines aspects of several of the English-language hymnals. This sampling, while not complete, explores the various genres of Roman Catholic hymnals available in the United States.

12.   I am referring here to work done by Walter J. Ong in *Orality and Literacy: The Technologizing of the Word* (New York: Routledge, [1982] 1988), pp. 38ff.

13.   There are many sources that speak of Taizé prayer. For a concise introduction see Brother Jean Marie, 'Prayer and Song in Taizé: Opening the Doors to an Inner Life', *Ecumenism* 31:124 (December 1996), pp. 16–18. A visit to the Taizé website <http://www.taize.fr/en/en_index.htm> might also provide additional background.

14.   Tracey discusses the nature of cyclic musical structure in 'Transcribing African Music in Pulse Notation', a monograph published by the

International Library of African Music, Rhodes University, Grahamstown, South Africa, 1997.

15. For example, the Praise and Worship phenomenon in the United States, highly influenced by charismatic worship practices, makes extensive use of cyclic structures or variants thereof.

16. Ronald Grimes, *Beginnings in Ritual Studies* (Lanham, MD: University Press of America, 1982), p. 44.

17. Tom F. Driver, *The Magic of Ritual* (New York: HarperCollins, 1991), p. 7.

18. Ibid., p. 100. Italics mine.

19. The charismatic-influenced songs of the contemporary Praise and Worship style often project the text onto an overhead screen, freeing the hands to clap or the body to sway. In practice, even this projection becomes unnecessary as the cycles repeat and the song is internalised. The oral (vs. literate) nature of these songs is further evident in that they are often learned by means of CDs or cassette tapes rather than through musical scores. Compact discs have become the electronic prayerbooks for Pentecostal and charismatic groups.

20. Op. cit., Ong, p. 38.

21. Ibid., p. 39.

22. Ibid., p. 41.

23. Ibid., p. 42. See Chapter 3, 'Some Psychodynamics of Orality', in *Orality and Literacy* for a more thorough discussion of the differences between oral and literate traditions.

24. *Music, Culture and Experience: Selected Papers of John Blacking*, ed. by Reginald Byron (Chicago: University of Chicago Press, 1995), p. 152.

25. Ibid., p. 153.

26. *Songs & Prayers from Taizé* (Chicago: GIA Publications, Inc., 1991), p. 29.

27. Daily prayer offices often benefit from a unified musical style and structure due to their brevity. Fuller services of Word and Table, by contrast, usually benefit from a diversity of musical styles and structures due to the greater length of the liturgy and the complexity and variety of ritual actions needed to sustain the liturgy.

28. Paul F. Bradshaw, *Two Ways of Praying* (Nashville: Abingdon Press, 1995), p. 65.

29. There are numerous examples from the writings of the early church that use congregational singing as a metaphor for Christian unity. Commenting on 1 Cor 34:5–7, Clement of Rome (fl. *c.* 96) urged Christians to join their praise with the multitude of angels in praise to God: 'Let us, therefore, gathered together in concord by conscience, cry out earnestly to [God] *as if with one voice,* so that we might come to share

in [God's] great and glorious promises.' See *Patrologiae cursus completus, series graeca,* ed. by J.P. Migne (Paris: 1857–66),1:276–277; trans. by James McKinnon, *Music in Early Christian Literature* (New York: Cambridge University Press, 1987), p. 18. Italics mine. Preaching on Ephesians 4:1–2, Ignatius of Antioch (*c.* 35 – *c.* 107) carries the metaphor further when he said: '. . . *it is that Jesus Christ is sung in your unity of mind and concordant love.* And to a [person] you make up a chorus, *so that joined together in harmony and having received the godly strain in unison, you might sing in one voice* through Jesus Christ to the Father, that [God] might hear you and recognize you through your good deeds as members of [God's] son.' See *Patrologiae cursus completus, series graeca,* 5:733–736; trans. by James McKinnon, *Music in Early Christian Literature,* p. 19. Italics mine.

30. Don Saliers, 'The Integrity of Sung Prayer', *Worship* 55:4 (July 1981), pp. 291–292, 293.

31. Miriam Therese Winter, 'Catholic Prophetic Sound', *Sacred Sound and Social Change: Liturgical Music in Jewish and Christian Experience,* ed. by Lawrence A. Hoffman and Janet R. Walton (Notre Dame: University of Notre Dame Press, 1992), p. 153.

32. For example, in the early Christian church catechumens did not receive an explanation for the ritual of baptism before they participated in its mysteries. The principle of mystagogical catechesis employed the concept of entering first into the baptismal act followed by a detailed explanation. Examples of mystagogical catechesis may be found in St Cyril's (*c.* 348) writings as well as others. See 'St Cyril of Jerusalem's Lectures on the Christian Sacraments,' trans. by R.W. Church, in James F. White, *Documents of Christian Worship* (Louisville, KY: Westminster/John Knox Press, 1992), pp. 158ff., for representative examples by Cyril, Ambrose of Milan, and John Chrysostom.

33. 'Constitution on the Sacred Liturgy' (1963), *The Liturgy Documents: A Parish Resource* (Chicago: Liturgy Training Publications, 1991), article 112. 'Valence' is a term primarily associated with chemistry. It refers to 'the combining capacity of an atom or a radical determined by the number of electrons that it will lose, add, or share when it reacts with other atoms.' *The American Heritage Electronic Dictionary,* 3rd edn., Ver. 3.0A (Wordstar International, Inc., 1993).

Amor Loci: Theory and Method in the Study of Christian Ritual Music

Helen Phelan

Introduction

Expressions of love are rarely called to share conceptual or actual space with academic discourse. It would be difficult to imagine the outcome of this encounter beyond the annihilation of one or the other. Yet this is the conundrum facing the liturgical or ritual scholar.[1] The liturgy of the Christian churches is rooted in 'the spiritual ideal of ceaseless prayer',[2] the continuous expression of praise and love by the created for its creator. An Irish manifestation of this is the *laus perennis*, 'a service of perpetual praise maintained by relays of successive choirs'[3] attributed to Columbanus. Liturgy, to appropriate Auden's words, is an *amor loci* of faith, a cauldron of activity within which love of God is given tangible, communal expression. It is anything but abstract: its colours, sounds, 'contours, strata and vegetation'[4] give voice, body and being to this love. Liturgical theology views this expression as a primary way of being with and knowing God, as *theologia prima*,[5] as a vital faith activity:

> People in love makes signs of love, not only to express their love but to deepen it. Love never expressed dies. Christians' love for Christ and for one another and Christians' faith in Christ and in one another must be expressed in the signs and symbols of celebration or they will die.[6]

A primary sign or symbol appropriated to this task is music. Singing, chanting and playing musical instruments are cross-cultural characteristics of religious ritual. The musicologist, liturgist or ritual scholar cannot approach the study of this sound without being cognisant of its role in what is fundamentally believed to be a corporate act of love. Objective methodologies will not encompass this activity. Nor will theoretical frameworks incapable of including the affective, the non-rational or the performative.

This short article suggests a theoretical and methodological framework for the study of Christian ritual music. The essential heart of the structure is the *behaviour*, or activity of music. The ritual *context* surrounding this behaviour is viewed from two perspectives; the *etic*, or 'outsiders' perspective of ritual studies and the *emit* or 'insiders' perspective of liturgical theology. The grounding of the model borrows from two theoretical communities: hermeneutic philosophy and interpretive anthropology with her musical daughter, ethnomusicology.

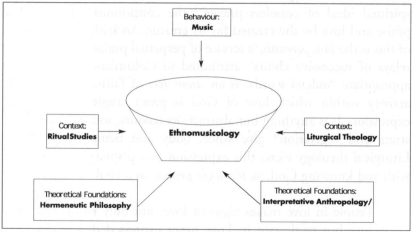

A Framework for the Study of Music in Ritual Context

The hermeneutic perspective

The primary contribution of the hermeneutic perspective involves the proposal that truth claims are interpretive. The pursuit of meaning at the heart of the hermeneutic enterprise takes any objective or absolute notion of truth as its first casualty:

> If there are only interpretations . . . of interpretations, then the
> systematic pursuit of 'truth' – 'truth' as the object of inquiry –
> or the search for axiological, epistemological and metaphysical
> foundations, will never be brought to completion. Is this not a
> central consequence of the hermeneutic circle, or, at the very
> least, of the chain of discourses and interpretations which
> identify and determine the hermeneutic circle.[7]

This does not put truth and interpretation in the opposing camps it
would seem to suggest. It does imply, however, that truth claims
emerge out of the dialogue process, the fusion of horizons implicit in
all encounters. Truth claims are not generated from an absolute
position but from a process of engagement with the text. This
involves a stance of humility concerning the adequacy of prejudice
and a willingness to engage with the hermeneutic circle of
anticipation, projected meaning and revision:

> [O]ne has to assume that a text has something to teach one
> and is a better authority on the subject-matter at issue than
> oneself . . . a relative independence from the effects of one's
> own initial prejudice is possible only under the assumption
> that the text has the authority to challenge the prejudice.[8]

Gadamer's insistence on the pursuit of consensus and the art of
agreement as primary prerequisites of truth claims is redressed by
Ricoeur's defence of critique and distanciation as necessary aspects of
the interpretive perspective. James Fodor notes the consistent
Socratic framework within which Ricoeur worked, one that insisted
on a balance between critical scepticism and doctrinal tradition. In
this sense, Christian hermeneutics involves a constant openness to
dialogue with God: a dialogue that values its Christian inheritance
without clinging to it with dogmatic adherence:

> If the community of God's people is to maintain itself in the
> truth (that is, escape the pressure of its own discourse to close
> in upon itself) it must surrender its speech to and thus derive
> the power of its language from that dialogue with the God of

Abraham and Jesus. Truth, in short, has a certain liturgical dimension.[9]

If truth is a cornerstone of faith, then Fodor suggests that the actions of faith, its rituals and behaviours may be the key to its experience. This truth experience, manifest in the rituals of faith, is the antithesis of Enda McDonagh's description of dogmatic theology as: 'A self-enclosed study of historical formulae and philosophical speculation without any of the impact of saving truth (*Heilwissen*) traditionally taken to be characteristic of Christian preaching and teaching.'[10]

If this description of dogmatic theology represents a closed and self-referential system of truth, liturgical theology and hermeneutic philosophy suggest a more radical claim, one based on the continuous meeting of experience with expression, of cultural interpretation and the humility of tradition in the face of new encounters.

It is in this sense that truth takes on a liturgical voice. Liturgy, by its nature, cannot exist in the abstract. It is more essentially actual than conceptual, more performative than dogmatic. Its manifestation is necessarily cultural in context and therefore always in need of interpretation. The concrete nature of its realisation means that it must be reckoned with anew in each time and place of its manifestation and that each of these encounters contributes to an understanding of its truth revelation. Music in liturgy may also be understood from this perspective. It is not an ornament, embellishing the proceedings, but a critical voice in the expression of the great Christian truth claim.

Interpretive anthropology

If hermeneutic philosophy provides some theoretical grounding for an understanding of music in liturgy as an ongoing and changing participant in the Christian dialogue of truth, anthropology has contributed both language and methodology to its expression. In *The Interpretation of Culture*, Clifford Geertz suggests that culture involves all expressive aspects of a primary human endeavour – the search for meaning. Religion and religious activity, its sounds and spaces, are all manifestations of this impulse. Meaning is unpacked through an understanding of the complexity of symbols formulating cultural experience: 'Believing, with Max Weber, that man is an animal suspended in webs of significance he himself has spun, I take culture to be those webs, and the analysis of it to be, therefore, not an experimental science in search of law but an interpretive one in search of meaning.'[11]

Music is a primary symbol of culture. The study of culture and of its symbols, according to Geertz, is best approached through the methodology of ethnography. Ethnography seeks to understand cultural symbols through the layering of a variety of activities including initial access to a community, the establishment of rapport and trust with its members, the selection of informants and interviewees for the variety of perspectives they may provide on the cultural activity, the recording and transcribing of interview texts, the maintenance of field notes and diaries as well as observation and participation in the cultural activity under scrutiny. This collection of perspectives facilitates the interpretive process through a recognition of its layered, complex and often paradoxical nature. Geertz adapts Gilbert Ryle's concept of 'thick description' to describe this: 'Multiplicity of complex conceptual structures, many of them superimposed upon or knotted into one another, which are at once strange, irregular and inexplicit.'[12]

It is not difficult to imagine the application of this methodology to ritual as a cultural activity and to music as one of the symbolic constituents of the ritual. Unlike traditional methodologies for ritual analysis, such as those that may have emerged from theology and musicology and may be driven by abstract considerations of 'good' liturgy or 'good' music, often with a Western, European bias, cultural anthropology suggests a methodology that is rooted in human behaviour – in this case, human ritual music-making – and is genuinely cross-cultural in its formulation.

If Geertz views ritual as an interesting example of cultural expression, Victor Turner suggests that it is in fact the primary manifestation of cultural expression as well as a forum for cultural change. Turner's work, particularly with the Ndembu of North-western Zambia, led him to an interpretive theory of symbol, closely linked to its ritual expression.[13] For Turner, ritual and its symbols provided the means with which a society seeks to define, re-define or recreate its self-identity. Through his exploration of ritual structures from the Roman Catholic Mass to the initiation rites of the Ndembu, Turner concluded that ritual symbols such as music provide a unique and ambiguous language for communicating complex social norms, attitudes and beliefs. Building on Turner's work, the ethnomusicologist Timothy Rice suggests that humans are born into a world of symbols, previous to understanding or explanation, and the hermeneutic enterprise involves both the embracing and rejecting of community and culture in an attempt to assimilate, interpret, challenge and grow.[14] The questions of religious rituals such as music-making are powerful agents in this process and strong carriers of communal belief systems.

Finally, more recent developments in anthropology and ethnomusicology have come to question the over-emphasis on all ritual activity as symbolic and in need of interpretation. This emphasis on meaning often shifts the focus from what is actually happening to what it is supposed to mean, viewing ritual as a 'text' in need of deconstruction and decoding. Theories of performance such as those of Pierre Bourdieu and Edward Schiefflin seek to redress this balance and restore the importance of performance for its own sake.[15] This development is particularly important for music as a symbol system that is not always easily 'interpreted' but whose performance is often central to ritual activity.

Ritual studies

In *Ritual: Perspectives and Dimensions,* Catherine Bell characterises contemporary thought within the discipline of ritual studies as hermeneutic, interpretive and performative.[16] She suggests three broad movements in the meta-history of this young discipline. The first is located in the so-called myth or ritual debate centred on speculation concerning the origin of religion. Nineteenth-century studies in comparative linguistics championed myth as the origin of religion while linguists such as William Robertson Smith argued for ritual, suggesting that religion did not develop primarily as an explanatory tool but as an activity to strengthen community bonds. The development of a phenomenology of religion through exponents such as Mircea Eliade shifted the emphasis back towards myth:

Eliade's approach also tended to place ritual on a secondary level, reserving a primary place for myth by virtue of its closer relationship to the underlying structures of all religious experience. Perhaps myth, as a matter of beliefs, symbol and ideas, is deemed a manifestation of the sacred that is inherently closer to the cognitive patterns that define *homo religious*, while ritual, as action, is considered a secondary expression of these very beliefs, symbols and ideas.[17]

The worlds of Freudian and Jungian psychoanalysis are also noted as sister disciplines to these early developments.

Whereas this first phase concerned itself with origins, the second developed a preoccupation with social function and structure. Bell notes the publication of Émile Durkheim's *Elementary Forms of the Religious Life* in 1912 as a benchmark in the establishment of religion as a 'social fact'. British anthropologists such as A.R. Radcliffe-Brown and E.E. Evan Pritchard explored the structures of this 'fact', including its rituals and associated behaviours. Others such as Turner and Geertz pushed beyond the mere pragmatics of its form and function to attempt a form of interpretation. Often referred to as symbolic-culturalists, they proposed highly developed theories of culture, symbol and ritual, as well as methodologies grounded in their own work in the field.

Bell concludes her survey by examining the emergence of performance theories, the latest school to recognise that meaning does not reside primarily in textual deconstruction but in its performative components such as music, gesture and drama.

While ritual studies is still articulating its own history, it is also seeking to define itself. Definitions of ritual can be broad enough to include any biologically or culturally patterned behaviour or narrow enough to be defined by a single denomination with exclusive reference to its own ritual activities. In *Beginnings in Ritual Studies*, Ronald Grimes is reluctant to offer any such fixed or 'hard' definitions of ritual but he does suggest six ritual 'sensibilities', one of which is liturgy. Grimes provides an interesting rehabilitation of the term 'liturgy' to refer to any ritual with a religious preoccupation:

> I do not restrict the term liturgy to Christian rites. Rather, it
> refers to any ritual action with an ultimate frame of reference
> and the doing of which is understood to be of cosmic
> necessity.[18]

Unlike other sensibilities such as decorum or ceremony, which
Grimes suggests are declarative and exclamatory, liturgy is defined by
its interrogative nature. Unlike magic, liturgy does not harness power
but waits upon it. Passivity or waiting in an attitude of receptivity is
a characteristic of liturgical acts as diverse as the Christian worship
and Zen meditation.

In many ways, ritual studies provides a point of intersection
between theology and anthropology, both being disciplines that
pursue knowledge of human behaviour and its attitude towards 'the
divine'. While it is true that religious studies also provides this
juncture, ritual studies is unique in that its primary preoccupation is
the ritual space and the activities within that space. It is primarily an
event-based discipline. It is uniquely dependent on the event context
of ritual. Similarly, ritual or liturgical music may exist without a
theology or theory of what it is but it cannot exist without
expression. Simply put, liturgical music can and does exist without
theology but not without music. This is as strong an argument as can
be made for the consideration of music itself as the necessary starting
point of any study, theory or theology.

Liturgical theology

Hermeneutics and interpretive anthropology provide the
philosophical attitude and interpretive frameworks of this model:
ritual studies sets the space for its performance. In engaging with the
final layer of this model, liturgical theology, the inquiry or academic
pursuit of ritual music enters the final frame, the inner sanctum.
While the previous layers provide a spectrum from, and a space
within which faith may be examined, only this final perspective
demands it. Liturgical theology, like any theology, is an inner voice,
not one necessarily incapable of dialogue beyond itself, but one that
recognises its point of departure as its own faith perspective. It is
perfectly possible to explore Christian ritual music without this

frame; such endeavour is regularly pursued within the disciplines of religious studies, ritual studies or ethnomusicology. If liturgical theology is to be included as a frame of reference it demands the grasping of the nettle of faith as well as its implications for any academic pursuit.

In *Liturgical Theology*, Aidan Kavanagh explores this highly charged ground within which faith and scholarship meet. He notes this tension as a relatively recent development connected with the pursuit and affirmation of 'objective' methodologies and results within research in the natural sciences. Earlier philosophical or humanistic pursuits that co-existed comfortably with concepts of faith followed the natural sciences away from the metaphysical towards the physical, empirical and observable. Subjective involvement, passion or belief came to be viewed as contaminating and suspicious. Kavanagh notes:

> The intellectual ecology all this seems to cause is curious. It requires that a mind which lives within this ecology work at a distance from whatever the mind addresses . . . [T]his is why what is done in divinity schools and seminaries is academically rather suspect, while what is done in departments of religious studies in state universities is not.[19]

While philosophy, anthropology and ritual studies have all embraced the hermeneutic stance as a possible and legitimate academic attitude, each in turn seems suspicious of entering into a 'fusion of horizon' with a faith-based position. Could it be that academic liberalism falls short of a spectrum this inclusive? Is the academic community suspicious to the extent that it modifies the hermeneutic enterprise to refer only to fusions that remain within the limits of subjective, negotiable, human knowledge?

Perhaps these limits would be acceptable if they did not significantly erode the researcher's access to a primary source of ritual information, that which is elicited within the domain of belief. Kavanagh likens this position to a tourist looking at an Indian reservation through a bus window:

Tourists on a bus to Santa Fe have access through their books and guides to more facts about the rain dance they are watching through their windows than do the Indians themselves. But the tourists can never really know the dance as the dancers know it, and knowledge alone does not make tourists Indians. Yet our intellectual ecology pushes us to accept more readily the tourists' than the Indians' sort of knowledge. Learned papers on the rain dance astonish no one more than the Indians.[20]

Embracing this final frame asks the researcher of liturgical music to be inclusive, not only of the activity of music-making, but of the faith of music-making within the ritual context. At the very least, a suspension of disbelief would allow the researcher a similar attitude of receptivity to that which Grimes suggests characterises liturgy itself. Perhaps it also rehabilitates the element of surprise within the academic enterprise.

Conclusion

While former research models may have emphasised the difference between theory (research) and practice (performance/ritual), the model suggested in this article is the result of an increased recognition that practice is a primary source for research and not an activity existing on a separate plane. In this sense, it should not surprise us that the starting point for research in liturgical music is the music itself. This model also reminds us that liturgical music cannot be fully understood outside of its ritual and cultural context and that the nature of the researcher's engagement with both context and behaviour is of primary significance.

The model brings the researcher through a circle of experience that begins and ends with musical behaviour. So central is the activity, so insistent the demand that behaviour has its own voice, before and after reflective translation, that it highlights the relative value of research within the world of music and liturgy. If, after all, music is best expressed through music, and ritual best understood through ritual experience, what is the value of a removed form of subsequent reflection?

The answer to this question is surely not absolute or singular. Just as the model presents a kaleidoscope of perspectives, all of which feed a 'thick description' of music in ritual, so too does it suggest that academic reflection and research is only a single vantage point, a single perspective on the world of music and ritual. It is a perspective that holds all the value of experiential data, a wide knowledge of context and the ability to remove, reflect, re-order and report. The musician values the particular vantage point of the musicologist but also knows that musicology is not music. Similarly, the liturgist, liturgiologist, ritual scholar or ritologist must always remember that ritual research is not the same as ritual. In fact, one might even suggest that this clarification is all the more important for ritual scholarship, since ritual so often seems to come into its own at precisely the point where rational language can no longer encompass the experience. Perhaps this is why ritual leans so heavily into the poetic to find its voice. Perhaps this is why Auden's description in 'Amor Loci' of sacred space as 'a love that does not abandon'[21] reveals an insight into the ritual forum that is impossible from the perspective of a theoretical model and method. Perhaps, where music and ritual thrive in partnership and community, these speak most naturally for themselves, out of themselves.

But this is increasingly not the case in the Western experience of Christian liturgy. The experience is one of decreased ritual sensitivity and decreased deployment of musical resources. It is increasingly possible to talk about 'ritual pathology'[22] as the primary religious ritual experience of the Christian West. Yet, even as this is happening, the rational and academic interest in religion is on the increase. In an article entitled 'History's Swollen Congregation' from the *Times Higher Education Supplement*, Simon Targett notes that:

> While devout vicars are preaching before depressingly puny congregations hardly deserving of a collective noun, hundreds of religious scholar-commentators are addressing packed academic conferences and filling high street book-shops and high class *bibliothèques*.[23]

This may well be an indication of two trends. It is reflective of the Western obsession with analytical ways of knowing and understanding. But it may also be one way in which the Western, rational, contemporary community can address the role and function of religion in its world and, by utilising models from ritual studies and liturgical musicology, may well come to the conclusion that religion and ritual have a unique role to play in human experience and the near impossible attempt to articulate, assimilate and survive our humanity.

Notes

1.   This article adopts Ronald Grimes's usage of 'liturgy' to denote rituals of a religious nature. See *Beginnings in Ritual Studies* (University of South Carolina Press, 1995), p. 51.
2.   *The Church at Prayer,* ed. by Aimé Georges Martimort, trans. by Matthew J. O'Connell (Collegeville, Minnesota: The Liturgical Press, 1986), IV, p. 157
3.   Peter O'Dwyer, *Towards a History of Irish Spirituality* (Dublin: Columba Press, 1995), p. 27.
4.   W.H. Auden, 'Amor Loci' from *The New Oxford Book of Christian Verse,* ed. by Donald Davie (Oxford University Press, 1981), p. 246.
5.   Kevin W. Irwin, *Context and Text: Method in Liturgical Theology* (Collegeville, Minnesota: The Liturgical Press, 1994), p. 45.
6.   The Bishops' Committee on the Liturgy of the United States Catholic Conference, 'Music in Catholic Worship', article 4 from *The Liturgy Documents,* ed. by Mary Ann Simcoe (Chicago: Liturgy Training Publications, 1985).
7.   *The Hermeneutic Tradition: From Ast to Ricoeur,* ed. by Gayle L. Ormiston and Alan D. Schrift (Albany, NY: State University of New York Press, 1990), p. 3.
8.   Georgia Warnke, *Gadamer: Hermeneutics, Tradition and Reason* (California: Stanford University Press, 1987), pp. 86–87.
9.   James Fodor, *Christian Hermeneutics: Paul Ricoeur and the Refiguring of Theology* (Oxford: Clarendon Press, 1995), p. 42.
10. Enda McDonagh, *The Making of Disciples: Tasks of Moral Theology* (Delaware: Michael Glazier Inc., 1982), p. 1.
11. Clifford Geertz, *The Interpretation of Cultures* (New York: Basic Books, 1971), p. 5.
12. Ibid., p. 10.

13. Victor Turner, *The Ritual Process, Structure and Anti-Structure* (New York: Cornell Paperbacks, 1977).

14. Timothy Rice, *May It Fill Your Soul, Experiencing Bulgarian Music* (University of Chicago Press, 1994).

15. Pierre Bourdieu *Outline of a Theory of Practice* (London: Cambridge University Press, 1973).

16. Catherine Bell, *Ritual: Perspectives and Dimensions* (Oxford University Press, 1997).

17. Ibid., p. 11.

18. Ronald Grimes, *Beginnings in Ritual Studies*, rev. edn. (University of South Carolina Press, 1995), p. 51.

19. Aidan Kavanagh, *On Liturgical Theology* (Collegeville, Minnesota: Liturgical Press, 1984), p. 10.

20. Ibid., p. 10.

21. W.H. Auden, op. cit., p. 246.

22. See Ronald Grimes's use of 'ritual pathology' in *Beginnings in Ritual Studies.*

23. *The Times Higher Education Supplement,* 5 July 1996, p. 15.

IRISH SPIRITUALITY AND MUSIC

EVIDENCE FOR MUSIC IN THE MEDIEVAL
IRISH LITURGY: A SURVEY

Barra Boydell

SOURCES OF LITURGICAL MUSIC are not plentiful from medieval Ireland, but what does survive allows for a general picture to be established of the forms and role of music in the liturgy of the later medieval Irish Church. Musical practices in the so-called Celtic rite of the early Irish Church, before the introduction of the Roman liturgy to Ireland in the eleventh and twelfth centuries, are less easy to reconstruct, however, since no clear examples of musical notation survive in any Irish liturgical sources from before the twelfth century. Nevertheless, despite Frank Harrison's assertion made in 1967 that 'the music of the Celtic rite has sunk without leaving a trace',[1] a number of surviving manuscripts do provide clues to musical practices in this earlier period.

The most significant of these are the seventh-century *Antiphonary of Bangor* (from Bangor, County Down);[2] the *Stowe Missal*, copied in Munster *c.* 800 from a manuscript dating from before 650;[3] and the *Liber Hymnorum* of the late eleventh and early twelfth centuries.[4] References in these and other early Irish sources to the singing of chants and hymns confirm that music formed part of the early Irish liturgy. The *Stowe Missal*, for example, refers to sections of the mass sung, apparently, by a group of singers,[5] and an addendum to a hymn to St Columba in the *Liber Hymnorum* includes the line 'While we sing hymns with grateful hearts' (the liturgical use of hymns is one aspect in which the Celtic rite differed from that of Rome).[6]

Although none of these manuscripts contains any musical notation, recent musicological research has begun to uncover some evidence for the music of the early Irish liturgy. Certain chants specific to Irish saints in later medieval Irish liturgical sources display unique melodic characteristics, which Patrick Brannon has suggested may represent survivals of the music of the Celtic rite.[7] Equally, the text of the hymn *Ecce fulget clarissima Patricii* from the *Liber Hymnorum* reappears with music in an early fifteenth century breviary.[8] Since the text pre-dates the introduction of the Roman liturgy into Ireland, it is possible that the music may represent a survival into the fifteenth century of an Irish melody dating from the pre-Norman Celtic rite.[9]

The earliest Irish liturgical source with musical notation is the *Drummond Missal,* copied between the later eleventh and mid-twelfth centuries, probably in Glendalough, County Wicklow.[10] Although clearly influenced by the Roman liturgy, which was being introduced into Ireland at this time, at least some of the chants in the *Drummond Missal* may be representative of the Celtic rite. The musical notation, however, consists of non-diastematic neumes. These are markings above the text indicating the shape of the melody and serving as memory aids for the singer. Although non-diastematic neumes do not indicate pitch or rhythm and cannot be transcribed directly into musical notation, the possibility of reconstructing chants from these neumes in the *Drummond Missal* is currently under investigation.[11]

Perhaps the most intriguing evidence to emerge in recent years for early Irish chant is in the form of forty-eight fragments of notated chant from Irish monasteries in south Germany and Austria, which have recently come to light from the Schottenstift in Vienna. The monks of these monastic communities were exclusively of Irish origin until 1418, when their order was taken over by German monks of the monastic order of Melk. It is thus very possible that the earliest of these fragments dating from the early twelfth and thirteenth centuries provide further evidence of native Irish liturgical musical practices.[12]

While the music of the early Irish liturgy remains elusive, though perhaps not entirely beyond recovery, there are some clues as to how it may have been performed. There are references to the antiphonal singing of psalms and also to the use of the *cruit,* a stringed instrument, to accompany chanting. Furthermore, historian and

musicologist Anne Buckley has drawn attention to the frequent
literary and iconographic sources from early Christian Ireland,
including high crosses, that refer to or illustrate monks not only
singing, but playing musical instruments.[13] Quite apart from the
actual melodies, the sound world of early medieval Irish liturgical
music may have been quite different from received views of how
medieval chant sounded, although it should be noted that Ireland is
not unique in providing evidence for the instrumental accompaniment
to chant in the early Middle Ages.[14]

Liturgical manuscripts with music survive in greater numbers
from the period following the introduction into Ireland of the
Roman rite (specifically the Sarum, or English version of the Roman
rite) in the eleventh and twelfth centuries. Although the Roman
liturgy must already have been in use in Dublin and other parts of
eastern Ireland that were linked directly with the southern English
Anglo-Saxon church,[15] the Sarum liturgy was officially adopted in
Ireland at the synod of Cashel in 1171–2. The fact that a synod held
fifteen years later, in 1186 at Christ Church Cathedral, Dublin,
found it necessary to declare its adoption within the diocese of
Dublin is a reminder that actual implementation could lag
significantly behind the issuing of decrees by synods.

Seventeen liturgical manuscripts and other sources of sacred
musical notation are known from Ireland between the twelfth and
the fifteenth centuries (see Fig. 1).[16] In some cases these contain
significant amounts of chant notation, in others only isolated
examples of music. For the most part they reflect the importation
into Ireland from at least the twelfth century of standard European
plainchant traditions, their melodies differing little from those found
in England and on the Continent.

The close links between Irish, English and continental liturgical
musical practices in the later Middle Ages are clearly reflected in the
few surviving examples of sacred polyphonic music from medieval
Ireland. A psalter known as 'Cormac's psalter', written in the middle
or second half of the twelfth century, includes a colophon (*Cormacus
scripsit hoc psalteriem ora pro eo . . .* 'Cormac wrote this psalter: pray
for him . . .') set for three voices using a *Benedicamus* melody of the
Sarum rite as the tenor, or lowest voice.[17] This is early in the

European context for three-part music. Also of particular interest, and indicating that Ireland did not stand apart from musical developments elsewhere in northern Europe, is a late twelfth-/early thirteenth-century gradual, thought to originate from the Benedictine monastery at Downpatrick (later a cathedral), that includes a short piece of two-part polyphony, the verse 'Dicant nunc Iudei' from the processional Easter antiphon 'Christus resurgens'. This is unique in the European context in providing the only known musical concordance for a polyphonic piece from before the later twelfth century, the same music occurring in a manuscript from Chartres dating from *c.* 1100.[18] This gradual also demonstrates links with Winchester, an important centre of polyphony in the early twelfth century.

Figure 1: *Musical sources for later medieval Irish sacred and liturgical music*

late 11th/ 12th cent.	Missal	**'Drummond Missal' – New York,** **Pierpont Morgan Library, Ms.m 627** Possibly from Glendalough, County Wicklow. Partially notated in non-diastematic neumes.
mid. 12th cent.	Psalter	**'Cormac's Psalter' – London, BL,** **Add.Ms.36929** Psalms and canticles without notation, but includes a polyphonic colophon whose Tenor is an adaptation of the Sarum chant 'Benedicamus Domino'.
12th/ 13th cent.	Missal	**Dublin, TCD, Ms.1305** Includes fragment of a notated missal of Irish Sarum Use.
late 12th /13rh cent.	Gradual	**Oxford, Bodleian Library, Ms.Rawl.C.892** From Downpatrick Benedictine monastery. Includes a two-part antiphon 'Dicant nunc Iudei' concordant with music from Chartres (*c.* 1100).
c. 1300	Antiphonal	**Dublin, Trinity College, Ms.82** Probably Irish Sarum Use. Bound with the Kilcormac Missal (dated 1458, but without notation).

c. 1360	Troper	**'Dublin Troper' – Cambridge, Univ.Lib.Add.Ms.710** From St Patrick's Cathedral, Dublin. Sarum Consuetudinary, Troper and Sequentiary; some Latin monophonic songs; sequences in honour of St Patrick; three settings (one monophonic) of 'Angelus ad virginem'.
14th cent.	Missalt /Sacred mote	**London, British Library, Add.Ms.24198** From Augustinian abbey of St Thomas the Martyr, Dublin. Binding includes fragment of a sacred motet dating before 1325
14th cent.	Psalter	**'Christ Church Psalter' – Oxford, Bodleian Library, Ms.Rawl.G.185** From Christ Church cathedral-priory, Dublin (Augustinian). Sarum use; the only musical notation consists of brief antiphons to some psalms; illustrated initials include monks singing and playing instruments.
c. 1400	Processional	**Dublin, Marsh's Library, Z.4.2.20** From church of St John the Evangelist, Dublin (Augustinian, ex Christ Church?). Sarum Use; includes notated liturgical drama *Visitatio sepulcri* and Proper processions for SS Patrick, Columba and Stephen.
c. 1400	Processional	**Oxford, Bodleian Library, Ms Rawl.Liturg.D.4** From church of St John the Evangelist, Dublin (Augustinian, ex Christ Church?). Sarum Use; includes notated liturgical drama *Visitatio sepulcri* and Offices for SS Patrick and Audoen.
early 15th cent.	Missal	**London, Lambeth Palace, Ms.213** Sarum rite, partially notated; includes Office for St Finian.
early 15th cent.	Breviary	**Dublin, Trinity College, Ms.80** From Kilmoone, County Meath. Includes notated Offices for SS Patrick and Brigid, in addition to regular Sarum chants.

early 15th cent.	Antiphonal	**'Antiphonary of Armagh' – Dublin, Trinity College, Ms.77** From Armagh Cathedral (vicars choral). Includes notated chants for St Patrick.
mid.15th cent	Antiphonal	**Dublin, Trinity College, Ms.79** Church of St John the Evangelist, Dublin (Augustinian, ex Christ Church?). Includes notated Offices for St Patrick.
2nd half 15th cent.	Antiphonal	**Dublin, Trinity College, Ms.78** For use at St Canice's Cathedral, Kilkenny, later used at Clondalkin, County Dublin, in 16th cent. Includes notated Offices for SS Brigid, Patrick and Canice.
late 15th cent.	Antiphonal	**Dublin, Trinity College, Ms.109** Irish Franciscan Roman Use; partially notated.
15th cent.	Missal	**London, British Library, Ms.Egerton 2677** Sarum rite adapted for Dublin practice; partially notated.

A mid-fourteenth-century troper from St Patrick's Cathedral, Dublin (known as the Dublin Troper),[19] includes a three-voice setting of the Annunciation hymn 'Angelus ad virginem'. Probably of north French origin, this hymn also survives in a number of different versions from France and England, the version from Dublin being the most elaborate. 'Angelus ad virginem' was widely known, and was even mentioned in Chaucer's *Canterbury Tales*. But the musical significance of the Dublin Troper does not rest solely on 'Angelus ad virginem'. The major part of this manuscript, the Troper itself (ff. 32r–131v), contains plainchant for the sung parts of the Ordinary of the Mass, which are frequently embellished with interpolated passages or 'tropes'. There are also sequences for various feasts including two in honour of St Patrick, and Marian sequences that are likely to have been sung at the votive Mass of the Virgin. While one of the two sequences in honour of St Patrick, 'Laetabundus decantet' (f. 101v–102r), uses the same melody as the Christmas sequence 'Laetabundus exsultet' (f. 41v), a widely disseminated melody probably of French origin,[20] the second, 'Laeta lux est' (f. 50v), is only known from two sources, of which this is the earlier, suggesting that it may have been composed in Dublin.[21] Also likely to have been composed in Dublin are thirteen of the Marian sequences for which this is the only known source, and a further eight for which this is the earliest recorded source.[22] While these chants possibly composed in Dublin are stylistically indistinguishable from other chants of the Roman liturgy, they do suggest the presence of an active school of plainchant composition in Dublin.

A fragment of a four-voice sacred motet of English origin dating from before 1325 was found in the binding of a fourteenth-century missal of the Augustinian canons proper of the abbey church of St Thomas the Martyr, Dublin. Three other fragments of the same motet, 'Rota versatilis', have been found in various contexts in England, and the complete music and text have been reconstructed from these four fragments.[23] Like 'Angelus ad virginem', this underlines the sharing of polyphonic musical traditions, especially between Ireland and England during the later medieval period. Also of interest, although not specifically sacred polyphony, are some fragments of (textless) musical notation, inscribed, probably in the later fifteenth century, onto pieces of slate found at Smarmore, County Louth.[24] Although consisting of only single, brief musical phrases, these examples of notation are of a type used for sacred polyphony, and may have been musical sketches for a polyphonic work, or a scribe's mere doodles. Nevertheless, the fact that these fragments came from a small church rather than a larger monastery or a major centre of population like Dublin suggests that more sophisticated polyphony may also have been sung in smaller and more isolated communities.

The similarities between the melodies of Irish Sarum chant sources and their English counterparts have been noted above and indicate how the music of the later medieval Irish liturgy was not significantly different from that in England. Nevertheless, some of the later medieval Irish musical sources have their own particular interest and importance. Two processionals dating from *c.* 1400 include the text and music for an Easter liturgical drama, the *Visitatio sepulcri*.[25] Both manuscripts came from the church of St John the

Evangelist, Dublin, which was adjacent to and served by the
Augustinian cathedral-priory of Christ Church, from where the
processionals may have originated.[26] While many elements of the
Visitatio sepulcri are common to other liturgical dramas known from
England and the Continent, this particular version may well have
been created in Dublin.[27] Attention has already been drawn to chants
in later Irish sources that are specific to Irish saints; while the
melodies of certain of these may conceivably retain elements of early
Irish chant, most are adaptations of plainsong melodies known from
English and Continental sources.

In conclusion, we can note that, while direct evidence for the
music of the early Irish liturgy is missing, a number of clues do exist,
including some melodies identified in later sources that may possibly
preserve aspects of pre-Norman Irish chant. Research into this
intriguing area of Ireland's music history is in progress. The evidence
from Irish Sarum sources of the later medieval period, following the
introduction of the Roman liturgy in its English forms during the
twelfth and thirteenth centuries, is much clearer. This emphasises
that, for the most part, the later medieval Irish church
enthusiastically adopted the musical forms of the English and
Continental Roman liturgy, although certain elements of early Irish
liturgical chant may have continued and been absorbed into the
Sarum rite. This would have occurred most particularly in the case of
certain chants associated with Irish saints, but Roman chant melodies
were also frequently adapted for this purpose. The limited evidence
we have for sacred polyphony in the medieval Irish church further
emphasises the close links with English and Continental traditions.
A visitor to Ireland during the later medieval period would not have
observed significant differences in the music of the liturgy from what
was familiar in other countries, except perhaps on certain feast days
of Irish saints when echoes of the former early Irish or 'Celtic' chant
may still have been heard.

Notes

1. Frank Ll. Harrison, 'Polyphony in medieval Ireland', *Festschrift Bruno Stäblein,* ed. by Martin Ruhnke (Kassel, 1967), p. 75.

2. Milan, Ambrosian Library, Ms.C.5 inf.

3. Dublin, Royal Irish Academy, Ms.D.ii.3.

4. Consisting of two books: Trinity College Dublin, Ms.1441 and Killiney, Dun Mhuire Franciscan Library, MS A2 (now in custody of the Archives Department, University College Dublin).

5. Patrick Brannon, 'Medieval Ireland: Music in Cathedral, Church and Cloister', *Early Music,* 28 (May 2000), p. 194.

6. Aloys Fleischmann, 'Celtic Rite, Music of the', *New Grove Dictionary of Music and Musicians,* ed. by Stanley Sadie, 20 vols (London, 1980), IV, p. 52.

7. Patrick Brannon, 'The Search for the Celtic Rite', *Irish Musical Studies, 2: Music and the Church,* ed. by Gerard Gillen and Harry White (Dublin, 1993), pp. 13–40.

8. Trinity College, Dublin, Ms.80.

9. Brannon, 'Medieval Ireland', p. 197.

10. New York, Pierpont Morgan Library, Ms. m. 627.

11. Sara Gibbs Casey, '"Through a glass, darkly": Steps towards reconstructing Irish chant from the neumes of the Drummond Missal', *Early Music,* 28 (May 2000), pp. 205–15.

12. Martin Czernin, 'Fragments of liturgical chant from medieval Irish monasteries in continental Europe', *Early Music,* 28 (May 2000), pp. 217–24.

13. Anne Buckley, 'Music and Musicians in Medieval Irish Society', *Early Music,* 28 (May 2000), pp. 185–6; 'Music in Ancient and Medieval Ireland', in *A New History of Ireland,* ed. by D. Ó Cróinín (Oxford, forthcoming), I.

14. Buckley, 'Music and musicians'.

15. Barra Boydell, 'Music in the Medieval Cathedral Priory', in *Christ Church Cathedral Dublin, A History,* ed. by K. Milne (Dublin: Four Courts Press, 2000), pp. 142–3.

16. This figure includes the *Drummond Missal* but excludes fragmentary sources such as the 'Rota versatilis' fragment and the Smarmore slates (see below); information in Figure 1 substantially based on Anne Buckley, 'Music and musicians'.

17. London, British Library, Add. Ms. 36929; illustrated and transcribed in Buckley, 'Music and Musicians', pp. 178–9; see also Françoise Henry and G.L. Marsh-Micheli, 'A Century of Irish Illumination (1070–1170)', *Proceedings of the Royal Irish Academy,* C, 62, no. 5 (1964), plate xlii; transcribed in Harrison, 'Polyphony', p. 78.

18. Oxford, Bodleian Library, Ms. Rawl. C. 892, f. 67v–68r; illustrated and transcribed in Buckley, 'Music and Musicians', pp. 180–1; see also Harrison, 'Polyphony', p. 78.

19. Cambridge University Additional Ms.710; facsimile edition: Hesbert, R-J, ed., *Le Tropaire-Prosaire de Dublin,* Monumenta Musicae Sacrae 4 (Rouen, 1966); See also W. Hawkes, 'The Liturgy in Dublin, 1200–1500: Manuscript Sources', *Reportorium Novum,* 2 (1958), pp. 33–67; G.J. Hand, 'Cambridge University Additional MS. 710', *Reportorium Novum,* II (1957–60), pp. 17–23.

20. Hesbert, *Le Tropaire-Prosaire de Dublin,* pp. 20 (n.6), 58.

21. Ibid., pp. 21, 60, 79f (transcription).

22. Ibid., pp. 21, 63–65; selected transcriptions and commentary, pp. 86–96.

23. London, British Library, Add. Ms. 24, 198; Margaret Bent, *'Rota versatilis:* Towards a Reconstruction', *Source Materials and the Interpretation of Music. A Memorial Volume to Thurston Dart* ed. by Ian Bent (London: Stainer and Bell, 1981), pp. 65–98, incl. transcription; facsimile: *Manuscripts of fourteenth century English polyphony,* ed. by Frank Ll. Harrison and R. Wibberly (London: Stainer and Bell for the British Academy, 1981), pp. 3–8.

24. National Museum of Ireland, accession nos. 1961: 12, 24, 34, 41; transcribed and illustrated in Harrison, 'Polyphony'; see also A.J. Bliss, 'The Inscribed Slates at Smarmore', *Proceedings of the Royal Irish Academy,* C, 64, (1965), pp. 33–60.

25. Dublin, Marsh's Library, Ms. Z.4.2.20; Oxford, Bodleian Library, Ms. Rawl. Liturg. d. 4; transcribed in: Maire Egan-Buffet and Alan J. Fletcher, 'The Dublin *Visitatio Sepulchri* Play', *Proceedings of the Royal Irish Academy,* C, 90, no. 7 (1990), pp. 159–241; see also Alan J. Fletcher, *Drama, Performance and Polity in Pre-Cromwellian Ireland* (Cork and Toronto: Cork University Press, University of Toronto Press, 2000), pp. 61–77, 281–301.

26. Fletcher, *Drama,* p. 77. The church of St John the Evangelist, in Fishamble Street, was demolished in the nineteenth century.

27. Fletcher, *Drama,* p. 62.

Some Dimensions of Early Irish Piety

Seán Ó Duinn

THE SCENARIO FURNISHED by the early Irish church in terms of monasticism, relations with Rome, liturgical rites of the official Church type and devotional practices outside the canonical liturgy is one of very considerable complexity. Some distinctions can be made, however, that may help to identify the broad outlines of the subject, while keeping in mind that particular periods and groups resist rigid differentiation.

Here, I am chiefly concerned with the early Irish church, or Celtic period, from its foundations in the fifth century to the coming of the Normans in the twelfth century, and its residues today. This is generally regarded as the period when the Irish were free from overt outside control, but it must be remembered that this early Irish Church was fundamentally a Roman church with certain native modifications. The official liturgy as presented in our two main manuscripts, the *Stowe Missal* (9th century) and the *Antiphonary of Bangor* (7th century) are in Latin, though some of the rubrics in the *Stowe Missal* are in Irish.

The bishop or priest as representative of the official Church had a certain international character. He looked to Rome as a vital centre of his calling. His priestly duties, including Mass, Office and administration of the Sacraments, were conducted in Latin, the language of the Roman empire and the western church, a language never spoken by the native Irish. Indeed, this may have contributed to the idea of Latin as a sacred language connected with the esoteric rituals of the liturgy, which in turn may have helped to develop the idea of the liturgy as a sacred action shrouded in an atmosphere of mystery. The loss of this sense of the sacred on a considerable scale

since the introduction of the new liturgy following the Second
Vatican Council is a cause of some dismay.

In the *Stowe Missal*, we have an example of an *Ordo Missae*, or
Ordinary of the Mass, for this period.[1] It represents the type of Mass
said in at least some parts of the country at that time. The
suppression of this and other usages of the Celtic church came with
the Synod of Cashel in 1172. From this point forward, the Sarum
Rite (Rite of Salisbury) was to prevail.[2]

For whom was the *Stowe Missal* meant? Naturally it was meant
for monastic communities of monks and clerics and the wider
monastic community of *Manaigh*, that is, the large body of men,
women and children attached to a large monastery as monastic
tenants. There were also the faithful in outlying areas who had a
church and a resident priest who celebrated regular Church services.

The *Rule* of the Céilí Dé – a monastic reform group of the eighth
and ninth centuries – lays down that priests be appointed and that
baptism, intercessory prayer for both the living and the dead, and the
Sacrifice of the Mass on Sundays and Holy Days be provided for the
monastic tenants.[3] In addition, a priest in charge of a church and
faithful was expected to celebrate the Canonical Hours daily. He
probably did this on his own, reciting the psalms aloud from a lectern
in the middle of the church as is done by devout Anglican priests
today for Matins and Evensong.

Outside of this organised ecclesiastical scene, however, there must
have been many Christians living in isolated areas unconnected with
a monastery or ecclesiastical centre except perhaps by way of a yearly
pilgrimage. It is doubtful that they would have attended regular
Sunday Services, and their piety would have tended to be less
ecclesiastically orientated and would have leaned more heavily on
pre-Christian beliefs and practices.

In contemporary Ireland, there are still some examples of this
distinction between the more ecclesiastical and the more native forms
of piety and the clash that sometimes occurs between them. On the
Saturday before 'Domhnach Chrom Dubh' (the last Sunday in July),
large crowds of people from all over Clare and the Aran Islands still
assemble at Dabhach Bhríde, the great shrine of St Brigid near
Liscannor, County Clare, to celebrate the rites in the traditional way

by doing the rounds, drinking from the Holy Well, holding lighted candles, and entertaining themselves with song and story through the night-long vigil.[4] On the period around the 1940s a commentator remarked:

> They left home on Saturday, held an all-night vigil at the blessed well and arrived home on Sunday. The strange thing about it was that those people didn't mind missing Mass on that Sunday as if the Round was more important.[5]

The celebration of an archaic ritual in a *neimheadh* or sacred grove at the Festival of Lughnasa marking the triumph of the generous god Lugh over the stingy harvest god Crom Dubh, or Balar of the Evil Eye, would, indeed, strike the devout, anglicised, Romanised Catholic of the mid-twentieth century as decidedly odd.

While the feast of St Brigid is at another great date in the Celtic Insular Calendar – Imbolc (1 Feb.) – Brigid may also be associated with Baoi (Boi), wife of Lugh. Their child is the corn, the wheat and barley by which we live, and the corn is just ripening at this first-fruits festival. Brón Trogain – the sorrow of the earth – is another name for Lughnasa, as the earth is suffering the pains of childbirth as it gives birth to the harvest.[6]

At the same period of Lughnasa, thousands of pilgrims are climbing Croagh Patrick to assist him in dispersing the Powers of Darkness, as he, after much prayer and fasting on the same mountain, had dispersed the demon birds,[7] just as Lugh before him had dispersed the dark evil gods of blight and tyranny – the Fomhóraigh – at the Battle of Maigh Tuireadh.[8] In these ancient ritual observances, a linking line of continuity can be seen between the pagan past and the Christian present.

We can distinguish then, to some extent, two different strata of Christian tradition in Ireland even before the Norman invasion with its Continental ecclesiastical system. The less Roman, more native form of Christianity is bound up with sacred sites such as Croagh Patrick, Lough Derg, Gougane Barra, Baile Bhoirne, Cnoc Bréanainn and the many pilgrimage sites and holy wells throughout the country. Rituals are performed at these sites on sacred dates of the Celtic calendar. The native folk worship tends to be outdoors – pilgrimages, doing the rounds at holy wells, bonfires on St John's Eve (23 June, the summer solstice), the Brídeog procession, etc.

There are many manifestations of this native folk worship, such as the great collection of *paidreacha dúchais* or native prayers in Ireland and Gaelic Scotland. These are short texts known by heart to be said in association with the various acts and situations of the day such as rising, going to bed, taking meals, or even sneezing. Some of these have a distinctly ritual character, for instance the texts for *Smáladh na Tine* – the covering of the fire with ashes at night and its revival in the morning; prayers for lighting the lamp; the *suantraí* or lullaby sung by the mother or grandmother to put a child to sleep. Others have enormous poetic beauty, such as the magnificent Scottish prayer, with its emphasis on the long 'U' sound, said by fishermen when looking at the moon:

> Glóir duit féin, a Dhé na nDúl,
> ar son lóchrann iúil an chuain,
> do lámha féin ar fheilm mo stiúir,
> is do rún ar chúl nan stuagh.[9]

> (Glory to you, O God of the Elements,
> for the shining lantern of the sea;
> may your hands be guiding my rudder
> and your mysterious love behind the waves.)

Lay baptism was common in the Hebrides, as some islands had no resident priest. The ritual employed differs greatly from that of the *Rituale Romanum,* and is of considerable interest.[10]

The native rituals are generally non-hierarchical, in the sense that no priest is required. In some cases the official church has added on the celebration of Mass to the pilgrimage rite. Most pilgrims welcome this but not all. I remember a local man complaining about an enthusiastic curate who was bent on introducing official church services in addition to the traditional rites. He remarked sourly: 'Tá sé ag iarraidh sinn a Rómhánú' (He is trying to Romanise us).

Generally there are no books, no hymns, no sermons, no vestments, except archaic corn costumes, elaborate headgear and masks required for certain rituals such as the Brídeog, Hunting the Wren, or Strawboys at Weddings. Short ritual formulae are recited by heart.

Sacred time

Rituals are performed on a saint's feast-day or on sacred dates on the insular Celtic calendar, such as Samhain (1 Nov.), Imbolc (Lá 'le Bríde, 1 Feb.), Bealtaine (1 May), Lughnasa (or Lúnasa, 1 August) and St John's Eve (summer solstice, 23 June).

At Brú na Bóinne (Newgrange) the rising sun at the Winter Solstice (21 Dec.) sends a shaft of light into the interior of the tomb-womb to light up the ashes of the cremated dead. On this very day the Advent 'O Antiphon' sung at Vespers addresses Christ as 'O Oriens' and invites him to 'illuminate those who sit in darkness and in the shadow of death' (O Oriens, splendor lucis aeternae, et sol justitiae: veni et illumina sedentes in tenebris et umbra mortis).

Brú na Bóinne is one of the great mystery sites of the world. Its construction is dated to around 3000 BC, almost 3000 years before the Celts arrived, according to common opinion.[11] Many ancient Irish stories, however, mention Brú na Bóinne, and 'Altram Tige Dá Medar'[12] and 'Tochmarc Étaíne'[13], and people it with Celtic gods and goddesses such as An Daghdha, Aonghus Óg, Midhir, Ealcmar, Bóinn, Eithne, Coirceog. The conclusion is that the Celts took over this sacred site of their Megalithic predecessors and filled it with their own deities.

If the newcomers took over a megalithic building, however, may it not be that certain echoes of the pre-Celtic Megalithic religion still resound in this ancient site? Perhaps there is a hint of the winter solstice phenomenon in Tochmarc Étaíne, where An Daghdha deceives Ealcmar into thinking that only a single day has passed when in fact almost a year has gone by, by which time An Daghdha and Ealcmar's wife Bóinn have a child.

Again, in the romantic story 'Tóraíocht Dhiarmada agus Ghráinne', the hero, Diarmaid, is killed by the magic boar of Beann Gulban and in turn kills it so that they die together. Then Aonghus

Óg, Lord of Brú na Bóinne, comes along and transports the body of Diarmaid to Brú na Bóinne on a golden bier with his spear above it. This happens, significantly, on the last night of the year ('an oídhche dhéidheannach don bhliadhain') and then Aonghus Óg makes his dramatic statement:

'Agus ó nach bhféidir liom a aithbheodhadh arís, chuirfhead anam ann ar chor go mbiaidh ag labhairt liom gach lá'.[14] (And since I am unable to resuscitate him again, I will put a soul into him so that he will be speaking to me every day.)

This enigmatic site holds on tenaciously to its mysteries but we may well wonder if the golden bier and spear taking the body of Diarmaid into Brú na Bóinne on the last day of the year is an echo of the sun entering the chamber at the winter solstice to 'enlighten' the dead and transfer them from the womb of the Earth Mother to another dimension so that they may walk and talk among the gods and ancestors. Perhaps a key to the meaning of Brú na Bóinne and related monuments is given by the famous Egyptologist Rundle Clark:

> The early agricultural peoples combined fertility rites with the cult of the dead. . . . The community was not merely composed of the living but of the ancestors as well. Life on earth was a temporary exile from the true, undifferentiated group – life somewhere beyond. The ancestors, the custodians of the source of life, were the reservoir of power and vitality, the source whence flowed all the forces of vigour, sustenance and growth. Hence they were not only departed souls but still active, the keepers of life and fortune. Whatever happened, whether for good or evil, ultimately derived from them. The sprouting of the corn, the increase of the herds, potency in men, success in hunting or war, were all manifestations of their power and approval. Hence the place where the ancestors dwelt was the most holy spot in the world. From it flowed the well-being of the group. Without the tomb or the cemetery, life on earth would be miserable, perhaps impossible.[15]

The winter solstice in Ireland is also marked by the rite of 'hunting the wren'. This may, like Newgrange, belong to the pre-Celtic, Megalithic period.

The wren, 'the king of all birds' representing human kingship and embodying community, is killed and taken from house to house, and each household contributes some money 'to bury the wren'.

The profound religious meaning of the rite is not well understood. The reigning king has come to the end of his period of office at the winter solstice and must for his people's sake submit to death. He must hand over willingly the life he has received from nature, so that nature may give back life generously in the younger body of his successor and in the renewed fertility of the earth. The wren rite is about 'paying back one's debt to nature'.[16]

In many places today, hunting the wren is mere pageantry with no wren, not even an artificial one. In this case the 'Mysterium' is absent. In the Christian Liturgy, this is the time when the old King Herod is presented with his potential successor but is reluctant to surrender his kingship.

Sacred sites

The traditional folk-rites are generally performed at a sacred place – a *neimheadh* associated with the patron saint. Sometimes standing stones (*gallán*), cromlechs, or cairns are a feature of the site, indicating a pre-Christian cult area.

Glencolmcille in Donegal, with its major 'Turas' or ritual pilgrimage in honour of St Columcille on 9 June, is particularly noted for some of its 'stations' being at or near megalithic tombs. This valley is dotted with such remains, and is cut off from the hinterland by the surrounding hills, indicating that both the Megalithic people and the saints entered the area from the sea.

'Stations' are often marked by standing stones around which the pilgrims walk *deiseal* (sunwise) three times, and are sometimes connected with the saint's life – the spot where he prayed, where he sat down to view the landscape, where he performed a miracle, where the demons turned on him, and so on. In this way the pilgrim honours his ancestor in the faith, and unites himself to him in the very area in which the 'psychomachia' or spiritual war took place.

This type of layout is typical also of St Brigid's Shrine at Faughart, County Louth, and Baile Bhoirne, County Cork, the Shrine of St Gobnat. The process is not unlike the Stations of the Cross.

Generally speaking, the traditional ritual at sacred sites involves a lot of movement – usually in the form of the *cor deiseal* or sunwise circumambulation of a sacred object such as a well, a tomb, a church, a standing stone, a cross, or a tree. This is often done three or nine times, with the pilgrims following each other in single file, keeping the sacred object at their righthand side.

The Greek writer Athenaeus, writing about the Celts over 2000 years ago, mentions this custom: 'they do reverence to the gods, turning towards the right' (kai tous Theous proskunousin, epi ta dexia strephomenoi).[17]

The opposite, or lefthanded turn *(cor tuathal)*, was practised at such places as Inishmurray, off the coast of Sligo, by turning the *clocha breaca* or cursing-stones against the sun to bring one's enemy out of the harmony of creation.[18]

This is the form employed at Mass at the incensation of the altar, and at funerals for the purification of the sanctuary by the dispersal of demonic forces, and by surrounding the altar with a protective ring of fire.

A simple form of holy well rite would follow something of this order:

1. The pilgrim approaches the well from the north.
2. He/she kneels on the step before the well and says the opening prayer:

> Go mbeannaí Dia dhuit, a Ghobnat/Bhrighid Naofa,
> go mbeannaí Muire dhuit, is beannaím féin duit.
> Is chugatsa a thánag ag gearán mo phéine
> is ag iarraidh cabhrach
> ar son Mhic Dé ort'
>
> (May God salute you, O Blessed [Name],
> May Mary salute you and I salute you myself.
> It is to you I come with my painful complaint

and asking help from you
for the sake of God's Son)

3. The pilgrim takes up nine pebbles as counters and begins the
   rounds of the well in silence or saying some Our Fathers and Hail
   Marys, according to local custom. At the end of each round *(cor
   deiseal)*, the pilgrim throws away a stone so that when the correct
   number of rounds has been completed, the pilgrim's hand will be
   empty. In other places, the method of counting is different and
   perhaps more archaic: at the end of each round the pilgrim traces
   a cross with a little stone on a monolith near the well.
4. When the rounds have been completed, the pilgrim makes a
   token offering – a comb, a holy picture, a rosary, a stone, a pen,
   something small – these will be seen on a stone shelf.
5. The pilgrim drinks the water three times.
6. The pilgrim takes a piece of cloth that has been in contact with
   his/her body and hangs it on the *bile* or sacred tree beside the well.
   By this means, disease is transferred from the person to the tree.
   The piece of cloth keeps on 'praying' after the pilgrim has
   departed.

At elaborate sites many more rounds are made, of the church, the
Saint's grave, and monoliths. Sometimes there are other rituals
involved, such as passing a special stone around one self, lying on the
saint's grave, rubbing a *Síle na Gig*, renouncing the world, the flesh
and the devil, and so forth. Sometimes the rite is performed while
fasting and barefoot. The pilgrim is in direct contact with the earth,
with stone, with water, with vegetation. Each pilgrim has to perform
each section of the rite. It is very physical, the emphasis is on
movement, which is often strenuous and ascetic.

While all forms of spirituality have as their aim the uniting of the
human with the divine, it is possible to distinguish different
approaches. The traditional Roman approach emphasises the
transcendence of God – God as being utterly different from us,
incomprehensible, unimaginable, infinitely distant from us. Just like
the Romans, the Celts also held that God was transcendent, and

indeed, we have a marvellous expression of this in the Preface of the *Stowe Missal.*

When the emphasis is on this approach, the institutional Church becomes very important, with its hierarchy, dogmas and various ministers acting as intermediaries endeavouring to link the human being with the God who lives an infinite distance away. The Celtic system, however, tended to put the emphasis on the immanence of God. God was very near, God was present in the world, involved in nature, filling everything, invigorating everything, enfolding everything. God is 'Dia na nDúl' – the God of the Elements, earth, air, fire and water. As St Paul says, 'In him we live and move and have our being' (Acts 17:28), though in this case he was quoting, not the bible, but the words of a pre-Christian pagan philosopher.[19]

As well as in the Bible, the Law and the Prophets (Reacht na Litre and Reacht na bhFáithe) and through the Incarnation, God, according to the Irish view, was revealed to humans in the Reacht Aigeanta – in nature, in the trees, the land, the storm, the seas, humans, birds, animals, seasons.

A tenth-century poem expresses the idea vividly:

> Achainím ort tríd an uisce,
> is tríd an aer glan anfach.
> achainím ort tríd an tine,
> achainím ort tríd an talamh.[20]

> (I beseech you [O God] through water
> and through the pure stormy air,
> I beseech you through fire,
> I beseech you through earth)

The gradual removal of veils from the bread and wine in the *Stowe Missal* may be a later symbolisation of this triple revelation.[21]

The large collection of folk prayers in Irish and Scottish Gaelic for the ordinary situations of life such as rising, going to bed, or seeing the sun or moon, helps to build up an awareness of the divine presence at the six points – north, south, east, west, above and below (Dia romham, Dia ar mo dheis, Dia I mo dhiaidh, Dia ar mo chlé,

Dia os mo chionn, Dia fúm). This was ritualised by the Céilí Dé communities by turning towards the four points of the compass, to the sky, and to the earth, while saying the Our Father and *Deus in adjutorium* at each point.[22]

A cosmic vision is expressed in such simple prayers as:

> Éirím suas le Dia, go n-éirí Dia liom,
> lámh Dé i mo thimpeall, ag suí is ag luí
> is ag éirí dhom.[23]

> (I rise up with God, may God rise up with me,
> the hand of God around me when I am going about my
> business and going to bed
> and getting up)

Religious texts in Irish and Scottish Gaelic often appear strange and baffling to the modern Catholic. They present a world in which protection is needed against the attacks of hostile spiritual forces; where the ancestors in faith – the multitude of saints and the heavenly host of angels – are invoked; where saints fight dragons and where the 'psychomachia' or spiritual war against demons rages. This is a world of movement, colour, drama and danger.

Behind some of these texts a pre-Christian background may be discerned. But another factor also arises, that of a primitive form of Christianity, very different from the more evolved and perhaps more domesticated version familiar to the devout Catholic of today. An example of this is the layout and contents of the ancient and enigmatic text 'Lúireach Phádraig' (St Patrick's Breastplate) which, apart from the native section on the forces of nature, may have its counterpart in an early version of the Litany of the Saints.[24]

It may well be that what has survived is an early, ascetic and vigorous form of Christianity. Today, the worshipper is often asked as he leaves the church: 'Did you enjoy the Service?' A pilgrim returning from Croagh Patrick or Lough Derg might more fittingly be asked: 'Did you survive the Service?'

Similarly, many Catholics today would feel uncomfortable with the 'Eviction-installation Formula' of the Rite of Baptism for Adults

in the *Rituale Romanum*, in which Satan is ordered out of the
candidate so that the Holy Spirit may take his place: 'Exi ab eo
spiritus immunde, et da locum Spiritui Sancto Paraclito'. (Go out
from him, impure spirit and make way for the Holy Spirit, the
Comforter).

The Celtic Rite

The two major remains of the so-called Celtic Rite are the *Stowe
Missal* (9th century) and the *Antiphonary of Bangor* (7th century).
The Ordinary of the Mass has a fixed Lesson (1 Cor 2:26–32) and
Gospel (Jn 6:51–57), both referring to the Eucharist. Between these
readings comes the elaborate Bidding Prayer 'Deprecatio Sancti
Martine pro populo'. The name of St Martin of Tours suggests that
it reached Ireland through a Gallican channel. The mixture of
elements from Ambrosian, Gallican and Mozarabic sources along
with the Roman Canon is indicative of a period of liturgical
diversity.[25] Some of the Rubrics – short ritual directions for the
celebrant – are in Irish, for example, *isund conbongar in bairgen* (Here
the loaf/bread is broken). The actual breaking of the bread took place
before the Our Father, not after it, as in the Roman Rite.

Psalm verses, short responsaries, and litanies are prominent in the
Ordo Missae and these may have been set to a simple chant requiring
only a single chanter. It is surprising that such a simple technique is
not used more frequently today in small churches lacking a choir.
Since the music does not survive, there can be no certainty of its
form.

It would appear, however, that the Celtic Mass did not attain the
ceremonial magnificence and musical elaboration of the great Sarum
Rite of the later medieval abbeys and cathedrals.

As regards singing at Mass in more recent centuries in the Gaelic
speaking areas, Úna Ní Ógáin in her great collection *Dánta Dé* gives
a number of short prayers to accompany different parts of the Mass,
as for instance, the Gospel:

> A Dhia na trócaire, níor leor duit
> ár dteagasc tré d'fháidhth',
> ná tré d'aspalaibh naofa

dá dhílse a ngrá.
Gur labhrais linn tré Íosa,
tré d'Aon-Mhac na ngrás,
a geineadh ó Mhuire Óigh
is a d'fhulaing a Pháis.[26]

(O God of mercy, it was not
sufficient for you to teach us
through your prophets and holy apostles,
however faithful their love.
But you spoke to us through Jesus,
your only Son of grace,
who was born of the Virgin Mary
and who suffered his Passion)

The author's friend Pilib Ó Bhaldraithe, of Mayo, remarked to her: 'Chualas na daoine ghá ngabháil ar nós crónáin'. (I heard the people crooning them). A *crónán* is a humming or singing in a low, indistinct voice.[27] An old saying illustrates the idea: 'Is ar mhaithe leis féin a dhéanann an cat crónán' (It is for its own satisfaction that the cat purrs). It does seem that this was not full-voiced hymn singing but crooning.

The same use of the *crónán* seems to have been in vogue in the Hebrides. Alexander Carmichael, the great collector of folklore, remarks on the morning prayer 'Ceum na Corach', said out of doors: 'If the people feel secure from being overseen or overheard, they croon, or sing, or intone their morning prayer in a pleasing musical manner. If, however, any person, and especially if a stranger, is seen in the way, the people hum the prayer in an inaudible undertone peculiar to themselves, like the soft murmur of the ever-murmuring sea.'[28]

The same word *(crónán bleoghain)* was used for milking-songs. Some cows became so accustomed to these that they refused to give milk if the milkmaid did not croon. Many of these were religious songs:

'Thig, a Mhuire, 's bligh a bhó,
Thig, a Bhríde, 's comraig í.

Thig, a Chaluim Cille chaoimh
's iadh do dhá láimh mu m' bhoin'.[29]

(Come, Mary, and milk the cow,
come, Brigid and protect her,
Come gentle Colm Cille and entwine
your two arms around my cow.)

Much archaic Scottish music seems to have been recorded by Dr Donald Munro Morrison. He used a notation of his own invention, however, which he did not live to render intelligible to others. This is extremely unfortunate in view of his profound knowledge of music and Gaidhlig.[30] Perhaps some enterprising musicologist of a sleuthing disposition may yet undertake to break the code.

Prayers or incantations in rhythmic verse with a strong beat, whose recitation might, perhaps, have been accompanied by the bodhrán, open up another avenue for investigation.

The 'Fire Spell' chanted by the great Munster druid Mogh Roith as he struggled magically to blow his bonfire northwards to drive the invading army of Leinster from their camp in Knocklong provides an example:

Suathuim tene, trethnach tren.
reidhfigh figh, feoighfidh fer.
lasair lonn, lor a luas,
rosia snas sruith neamh suas.
cnaifid fech, fegha fuinn,
claifid cath, ar clann Cuinn.[31]

(I knead a fire, powerful, strong;
it will level the wood, it will dry up grass;
an angry flame, great its speed
it will rush up, to the heavens above;
it will destroy forests, the forests of the earth,
it will subdue in battle the people of Conn.)[32]

A Christian incantation against the disease of the Evil Eye provides a similar example:

> Cuirim an oba seo ri m'shúil,
> Mar a d'dh'orduich Righ nan dúl,
> Oba Pheadail, oba Phóil,
> Oba Shéumais, oba Eoin,
> Oba Chaluim-chille chaoimh,
> Oba Phadra sár gach naoimh,
> Oba Bhríde bhith nam ba,
> Oba Mhoire mhín nan ágh,
> Oba tromla [bó], oba treuid,
> Oba lomra [caorach], oba spréidh,
> Oba nolla [maithe], oba ní,
> Oba sona, oba síth,
>
> (I place this spell to mine eye,
> As the King of life ordained,
> Spell of Peter, spell of Paul,
> Spell of James, spell of John,
> Spell of Columba benign,
> Spell of Patrick, chief of saints,
> Spell of Bride, tranquil of the kine,
> Spell of Mary, lovely of the joys,
> Spell of cows, spell of herds,
> Spell of sheep, spell of flocks,
> Spell of greatness, spell of means,
> Spell of joy, spell of peace.)[33]

A well-known Irish Passion Prayer follows the same pattern:

> A Rí na gcréacht 'fuair éag I mbarr an chrainn
> is croí do chléibh' á réabadh ag láimh an daill
> is fuil do ghéag ag téachtadh ar lár 'na linn,
> ar scáth do scéithe beir féin go Parthas sinn.[34]

(O King of Wounds who died on the top of the tree
and the heart in your breast being stabbed by the hand of the
    blind man,
and the blood of your members flowing to the ground in a
pool;
on the shadow of your shield bring us to Paradise.)

Perhaps this type of rhythmic text might be included within the category of Ritual Chant.

This short examination of early Irish piety and its relationship with time, sacred space and ritual, reveals the combination of a creation consciousness springing from a rural civilization's experience of the earth with salvation history as presented by biblical narrative.

Notes

1.   P. Warren, *The Liturgy and Ritual of the Celtic Church* (Oxford, 1881), pp. 226–248.
2.   Ibid., p. 11.
3.   E. Gwynn, 'The Rule of Tallaght', *Hermathena*, No. XLIV, Second Suppl. (1927), 79–81.
4.   M. MacNeill, *The Festival of Lughnasa* (Dublin, 1982), Part I, 275ff.
5.   Irish Folklore Commission; Ms. 901,14.
6.   'Tochmarc Emire', in Van Hamel, A., *Compert Con Culainn and Other Stories* (Dublin, 1933), 43.
7.   MacNeill, op. cit., Part 1, 72–73.
8.   E. Gray, *Cath Maige Tuired* (Dublin, 1982)
9.   A. Carmichael, *Carmina Gadelica* (Edinburgh, 1940), III, no. 305.
10. Ibid., III, 2–3; nos. 217–221.
11. C. O'Kelly, *Illustrated Guide to Newgrange* (Wexford, 1971), p. 66.
12. *Érui*, XI, Part 2 (1932), pp. 184ff.
13. G. Gantz, *Early Irish Myths and Sagas* (Penguin Books, 1981), pp. 39ff.
14. P. Ó Canainn, eag., *Diarmuid agus Gráinne: An Giolla Deachair; Bodach An Chóta Lachtna* (Baile Átha Cliath, 1939), pp. 52, 62.
15. R.R. Clark, *Myth and Symbol in Ancient Egypt* (London, 1959), p. 119.
16. S. Muller, 'The Irish Wren Tales and Ritual', *Béaloideas* (1996–97), pp. 131ff.
17. J. Tierney, *The Celtic Ethnography of Posidonius* (Dublin, 1960), pp. 225, 247.
18. P. Heraughty, *Inishmurray* (Dublin, 1996), p. 32.

19. S. Ó Duinn, *Where Three Streams Meet* (Dublin, 2000), pp. 10–11.
20. S. Ó Duinn, *Orthaí Cosanta Sa Chráifeacht Cheilteach* (Maigh Nuad, 1990), pp. 64, 183.
21. Warren, op. cit., pp. 255, n. 29.
22. S. Ó Duinn, *Where Three Streams Meet,* pp. 78–80.
23. D. Ó Laoghaire, *Ár bPaidreacha Dúchais* (Baile Átha Cliath, 1975), Uimh. 8.
24. S. Ó Duinn, *Orthaí Cosanta Sa Chráifeacht Cheilteach,* pp. 163–165
25. Warren, op. cit., p. 204.
26. U. Ní Ógáin, *Dánta Dé,* (Baile Átha Cliaith: Ó Fallamhain, Teo., 1928)
27. P. Dinneen, *Foclóir Gaedhilge agus Béarla* (Dublin, 1927), p. 270.
28. Carmichael, op. cit., III, no. 229.
29. Carmichael, op. cit., I, nos. 93; 99.
30. Carmichael, op. cit., I, no. 5.
31. Ó Duinn, *Orthaí Cosanta Sa Chráifeacht Cheilteach,* p. 119.
32. S. Ó Duinn, *Forbhais Droma Dámhgháire/The Siege of Knocklong* (Cork, 1992), p. 99.
33. Carmichael, op. cit., II, no. 150.
34. Ó Laoghaire, op. cit., Uimh. 402

GREGORIAN AND ORTHODOX CHANT
– PERSONAL PROFILES

WESTERN PLAINCHANT

A Profile of Katarina Livljanic

What are your earliest memories of chant and of your desire to be a singer?
My memories stem from a very early age and are rooted in my experiences of childhood. I spent my early years in the Dalmatian city of Zadar, which was home to an early music festival. So, from a young age, my ears were exposed to the sounds of medieval music and I had the opportunity to hear many specialist ensembles as a very young child. I can say that from the age of about ten years my later vocation and resolve to dedicate myself to medieval music was already ripening.

Can you trace the steps of your journey as a professional singer and academic?
As I mentioned, I had a strong sense of clarity from a very young age about how I wished to dedicate my professional life. This early conviction eventually translated into the study of musicology in Zagreb and then later in Paris. At the same time, I had to pursue vocal training and worked with several specialists involved in medieval music. My main teachers in France were Marie Noël Colette in musicology, and Brigitte Lesne in voice studies. My journey with chant and early music has always included both singing and study. As well as these studies, I have had many very enriching contacts with various musicologists and singers interested in Latin liturgical repertoires.

What is your involvement in the chant programme at the Irish World Music Centre?
I was appointed director of the Chant programme in 1998 and was fascinated by the idea of a programme in chant performance

happening within the context of a country with a very vibrant indigenous music tradition. My appointment to the Sorbonne and the development of the chant programme to include a second stream in ritual song led to my withdrawal from full-time involvement and a restructuring of the original programme, but I am still very involved in the direction of the chant stream.

I believe that this course is one of the extremely rare programmes combining chant research and performance interpretation. It seems to me that it is impossible to enter the world of medieval chant without being conscious of its musical complexity and of the vocal skills necessary to perform the repertory. In some ways, it reflects something of my own journey, which has always seen chant scholarship and performance as things which must go hand and hand.

I saw the Irish World Music Centre as a place that could also stress a very precious link between chant and some layers of the traditional music repertory. This is possible, not only because Ireland still has a vibrant oral tradition of song, but also because a place like the Irish World Music Centre is experienced in the challenges of integrating oral transmission into academic contexts.

What is your interest in the connection between traditional singing and chant interpretation?
As a Croatian, I come from a country where traditional chant has been a part of the liturgy since the Middle Ages and is still sung today. The repertoire that we call Glagolitic chant has been written and performed throughout the centuries in the Slavonic language, even though Croatia belonged to the Latin Roman rite. This is a very unique phenomenon. In Dalmatia, the liturgy in the Middle Ages was, in a way, 'bilingual'. There were some churches where offices were celebrated and chanted in Latin, and others where it was in the vernacular in a very different style, but with equal musical complexity.

This unique inheritance has always interested me. I have worked a lot with traditional cantors and my experiences with these traditional singers and with oral transmission has helped me in thinking about medieval chant. I never try to imitate traditional cantors literally. I think that this would not lead very far – it would be more like a picturesque short-cut through a very complex musical landscape. But I try to understand the ways in which traditional chant repertoires are memorised and transmitted in cultures where the oral transmission is the basis, just as it would have been during many centuries of the Middle Ages. This is part of my interest in the chant programme in Ireland where the oral tradition is still so strong.

In the end, I try to develop a style in chant interpretation that combines many factors. These include the study of medieval manuscripts, modal language, rhetoric and this awareness of oral transmission.

Could you talk about your chant ensemble, Dialogos, *and your views on different forms of chant interpretation?*
A meditation about different forms of chant interpretation would need not only a whole book, but a whole lifetime to explain, and that is one of my main fields of interest! It is very hard to talk about it in a concise way, especially because there are many, many different 'chants'. There were many local repertoires in medieval Europe. There is what we call 'Gregorian' chant, which was not performed the same way in every place or during every century of the Middle Ages, and there is also the Gregorian chant used today in the liturgy, a completely separate phenomenon. All of these realities generate different performances, since they are all witnesses of different human realities in history.

But let me talk about *Dialogos.* The ensemble specialises mainly in Southern European liturgical music. At the moment, we are working on programmes of Gregorian, Beneventan, Glagolitic chant and early polyphony. It is an a cappella ensemble, which tours successively through many European countries and is nourished by my musicological research and by the dedication and enthusiasm of my singers. Our first recording, *Terra Adriatica,* focused on Croatian and Italian medieval sacred music.

What do you feel about the future of chant within liturgy?
This is a very difficult question for me because I am a very bad prophet! But it is also difficult because I am interested mainly in

medieval chant. The Second Vatican Council has changed many aspects of the presence of chant in the liturgy, and it survives today I think only in communities that are particularly interested in it. It is very difficult to impose a musical repertoire in the liturgy, and in this way, chant will survive and be performed only by those communities who really form a relationship with its sound. The style of its performance cannot be uniform, simply because people are not uniform. There is an influence of both the nineteenth-century musical taste and the restoration of chant during the twentieth century in certain monasteries, but this is just one of its faces. There are many countries and many styles of Gregorian chant performance in the liturgy today. The only thing we shouldn't forget is the fact that chant is a very complex musical repertoire and that it needs a very serious musical approach. And, above all, we shouldn't forget, that chant is very beautiful music.

BYZANTINE CHANT

A Profile of Ioannis Arvanitis

How did your interest in Byzantine music begin?
My name is Ioannis Arvanitis and I was born in 1961 in Stropones, a small village in the island of Euboea in central Greece. I was in the fifth class of elementary school when I stood for the first time with the singers in the church. Our teacher in the elementary school, Lucas Anagnostopoulos, had an excellent voice and was a church singer with a practical knowledge of singing, although he didn't know how to read musical notation. He didn't teach us anything specifically but we had the chance to sing with him – or believe that we sang! – and feel that we were members of the choir. This was my first contact with Byzantine music and church singing. I had no idea at that time that this was called 'Byzantine music' or that it has a special musical notation.

I went to the high school and started to learn western music and notation. When I was in second year, our music teacher, Spyridon Simitzis, who was and continues to be a Byzantine music teacher and singer as well, told us that we could learn Byzantine music with him. So I started to learn Byzantine musical notation, theory and praxis and at the same time I sang with him in the church. I stayed with him almost seven years singing in every service and helping him. In 1981, I acquired a 'Church Singer's Diploma' under his guidance. In the course of this time, I had already realised that what I had learned was not enough to explain the various ways of singing the Byzantine melodies. It couldn't explain the ornamental style of some singers or their so-called 'arrangements'. I had been taught to sing the notation almost at face value without adding many ornaments. On the other hand, although I liked ornamental singing and little by little became used to it and could even compose new melodies in this style, I was not satisfied with the concept of 'arrangement', which is what the followers of this style called the writing down of their performances. This simply meant writing down every note they used to sing, including writing the ornaments in full. But I liked the older way of writing and the older melodies. So, which was the correct way?

Eventually, I realised that the answer to my question was the doctrine of Simon Karas, a researcher with an enormous corpus of work on Byzantine chant, its theory and musical palaeography, as well as on Greek folk songs. In May 1982, I joined Karas's pupil, Lykourgos Angelopoulos, and began to sing under his direction in his Greek Byzantine Choir. In October 1982, I went to Simon Karas's music school to study with him. He was a somewhat difficult person and didn't want to accept all my previous knowledge and experience, not even that which I had gained with his pupil! So, he obliged me to begin from scratch! I stayed there for six years. Karas appreciated my abilities and my devotion to Byzantine and Greek folk music, so he trusted me to teach in his school from the third year of my apprenticeship with him. I taught there for four years.

How did your life as a professional singer of this repertoire develop?
As I have already said, I sang with my first teacher for almost seven years. With him, I acquired the practical knowledge of the liturgy and the services as well as of a lot of practical details of singing. I used to attend every service in the church, from beginning to end, and I became my teacher's principal assistant, singing sometimes in his place. In February 1982, I became for the first time a professional church singer, occupying the position of the (second) left singer at St Paraskevi's Church in Halkis, the capital of Euboea. I stayed there for four years. After some time, I became first singer for one year at St John's Church in the same city. I didn't occupy any other singer's position for some years but I used to sing as a guest in several churches in normal and whole-night services – in church singers' jargon, I became a 'sniper'! In October 1993, I undertook the directorship of the left (second) choir of the Church of Saint Irene at Aiolou St. in the centre of Athens, with Lykourgos Angelopoulos in the right (first) choir. I stayed there for six years. Because of some disagreements in

singing style, I was obliged to leave this church, so I became first singer in another church and stayed there for five months.

As well as singing professionally as a liturgical singer, I am active is the direction of Byzantine choirs for public concerts. I have been a member for many years and then the director for two years of the Choir of the Society of Church Singers of the Euboea Archdiocese. After I began to teach (1988) in the Experimental Public Music School of Pallini, in the district of Athens, I directed concerts with the pupils' choir in Greece and in the Abbaye of Royaumont in France. I have also directed the Greek Byzantine Choir in transcriptions made by me from old musical manuscripts. In the course of my teaching in the Model Musical Center of Piraeus (1994–1999) and the Philippos Nakas Music School (1999 up to this day) I managed to form a choir with my pupils and give many concerts in the frame of these music schools or in public. This choir is now becoming a professional one under the name 'Hagiopolites', and is going to publish an already recorded CD with monastic chant of the Mount Athos oral tradition. Hagiopolites will also give several concerts in the beginning of 2002 in Holland and Belgium.

My own international singing career includes many different chant repertoires. In 1997 I sang with Marcel Peres in concerts with the repertoire of Notre Dame. In January 2001 I participated in Old Roman Chant and directed my own transcriptions from old manuscripts in concerts with Alexander Lingas's 'Capella Romana' in Portland, Oregon, and in Seattle.

What are your primary research interests in Byzantine chant?
In 1982 I came in contact with Byzantine musical manuscripts for the first time. I began to study the old notation, which was used prior to 1814, when the Reform of the so-called 'Three Teachers' provided us with the current system of notation. This old notation was, and continues to be, rather unknown to the majority of the church singers and, even if some have a little knowledge of its profile, they don't possess a deep understanding of it. I can claim that I am almost self-taught in this field; I mean that I had no personal guidance except for the transcriptions of the Three Teachers, my knowledge and experience of the new notation and chant, and the doctrine of my

teacher, Simon Karas, described by him in outline and through some examples in three papers – he didn't teach me or any other directly about this. He was the first to investigate the old notation in a precise manner and suggest some fresh ideas about the meaning of the musical signs. At the same time, he proposed an interpretation (transcription) of some chants that differs from that of the Three Teachers. The Byzantine musical notation has a long history and its interpretation (especially the notation of the older chants) has been a matter of controversy among Greek and Western scholars.

The primary problem is the following: chants like the so-called 'stichera' (liturgical chants with psalmic verses before them) have a syllabic appearance in the manuscripts, i.e., to each syllable of the poetical text there corresponds in most cases only one or a very small group of musical signs and consequently, as it is reasonable to imagine, one or a very small group of notes. This was exactly the way Western scholars like E. Wellesz or H.W. Tillyard transcribed these chants. But the Three Teachers have given a highly melismatic interpretation of them, where to each old sign there corresponds a very large number of signs, and consequently of notes, in their new notation. This results in a stenographic conception of the old notation, i.e., the written chain of signs gives only a skeleton of the melody, which must be 'filled in' through an oral, but more or less concrete, tradition to give the full melody. In other words, the old chants were, according to the tradition of the Three Teachers, extremely long.

This interpretation, however, conflicts with a reasonable duration of the services, even according to medieval standards! So, the long way of interpretation could possibly be the tradition that the Three Teachers had received from their immediate forerunners, but it couldn't be the case for some centuries before them. The long interpretation is certainly not something imaginary, something coming from the mind of the Three Teachers, it's a fact, it's a tradition, but it must probably be, for one reason or other, a somewhat later one. My teacher, Simon Karas, investigated the notation of the old 'stichera' and proved that many of their formulas are also contained in another kind of chant, the 'heirmoi'. But the heirmoi were transcribed by the Three Teachers and are sung today in a syllabic or, sometimes, in a 'short melismatic' style, i.e., mostly with two time units and short melismas (a few faster notes) per syllable. In the same short melismatic style (and transcribed by the Three Teachers) the new stichera from the eighteenth century are also sung. So, Karas suggested that the old stichera should originally have a shorter interpretation and that they are in fact the ancestors of the currently sung stichera, revealing at the same time a continuity in the tradition in a process of transition from more complex to simpler musical forms. And this was not a mere suggestion. He gathered all the available evidence and managed to reconstruct the short melismatic interpretation of the old stichera, making this relation and continuity evident in a concrete manner. This has been also my own field of investigation. I found much more evidence in favour of this theory, organised this in a demonstrative manner and presented a paper in a symposium in 1993. But, as I will further explain, it is not a closed subject for me. I am still collecting evidence and researching in this field.

In November 1993, one day before presenting my aforementioned paper, I received a thirteenth-century published manuscript containing the music of the heirmoi. The text of these chants is still used today but the music is not the same. As I have already mentioned, heirmoi are sung today in two ways: syllabic and short melismatic. No other Greek scholar had, or has up today, given transcriptions of the heirmoi of the medieval periods. The style of the heirmoi of the thirteenth century or before is exactly the same as that of the old stichera. So, if the Three Teachers had transcribed them, they would have done so in a long melismatic way. This would be completely unreasonable, however, because heirmoi are only the musical patterns of long hymns with many musically similar stanzas. So, their music should have a shorter duration and their notation should be read in a syllabic or short melismatic way. Because of their similarity to the old stichera, it was reasonable for me to suppose that they should be interpreted in the short melismatic style already suggested by Simon Karas. I had worked on this some time ago but I wasn't completely satisfied. When I received the thirteenth century manuscript, in a moment's inspiration, I realised that not only heirmoi but also stichera should have a syllabic original form. This was of course not a completely new idea. Western scholars had already transcribed these chants in this way, reading the notation 'at face value'. There was one difference, however: they transcribed them either without a rhythm, even without a beat, or without a well-defined or mixed rhythm, according to their individual idea about the durations of the musical signs and their combinations.

The earlier scholars, like Wellesz or Tillyard, imagined that Byzantine chant should sound like Gregorian chant as sung by the Solesmes monks – free and oratorical. They couldn't accept that a medieval chant could have a specific rhythm or at least a well-defined beat. This could, of course, be true for Gregorian chant, but why should it be the case for Byzantine chant, too? This prejudice is very often present up to today.

Other later western scholars, like Joergen Raasted, tried to approach the subject by means of the present-day conception of the rhythm of Byzantine chant, i.e., the accent-based mixed rhythm that the church singers believe holds true for the chants they sing. But his, or other scholars', interpretations suffered from incorrect interpretations of the duration of some signs or of their combinations. So, my difference from the western scholars was that I realised that the old heirmoi and stichera should have a basically binary rhythm (or pulse) with very few exceptions of triple rhythmical feet, which, moreover, were usually present at very specific points of the chants. Central to this conception of rhythm is the fact that an accented syllable can fall on the upbeat, if it is on a higher note than at least one of its neighbouring syllables, i.e., if it has a pitch accent. This is in opposition to the current view of the singers who believe that an accented syllable must always fall on the downbeat (accent-based rhythm). This is sometimes applied in present-day chants, but no one has paid attention to it. I knew about it but I didn't realise that it could be of crucial importance. It seemed to impose itself on the music of the old heirmoi.

After this discovery, I managed to formulate a full theory of the rhythm of the old stichera and heirmoi, a theory that explains not only the composition of the music of these chants but also the construction of their contrafacta, i.e., of similarly sung poetical texts. So, not only the music is revealed in its more or less original syllabic and rhythmical form but an unsolved problem of hymnography, the problem of the meter of the poetical texts, is solved. Byzantine hymns appear mostly as prose texts in the liturgical books, so their poetical nature was doubted. My investigation showed in a concrete way that although they are in fact like prose, they acquire a meter through the musical setting and this 'musical meter' is the basis for the construction of the poetical texts of the contrafacta. The results of this investigation can be applied to the contemporary chants, which are the descendants of the older ones, leading to a full and deep understanding of the rhythm and of the continuity and transformation of chant in the course of time.

What I have said is related to the first stages of the notation, and the chants written down by means of it. But the notation and the chants themselves bear a continuous evolution. All this is part of my research because I believe in a diachronic study of Byzantine chant. One cannot solve problems of the present-day praxis and theory without referring to the past and, inversely, the present-day praxis can give at least an idea of some aspects of the past. I have seen how a mere synchronic study has very often led to errors and misconceptions.

Another field of my investigations is the study of the history of the modes. The same poetical texts have remained in use in the church for many centuries, but little by little their music has changed. Although heirmoi, for example, were written down at some point in time (musical manuscripts date from the tenth century), their liturgical use as model melodies for other chants forced singers to rely chiefly on their memory rather than on the written melody. So, heirmoi became essentially a part of the oral tradition, occasionally written down but already in a form transformed by orality. This process of transformation applied even to a change of the scales or the tonic of some modes. Studying all these stages of the music of the chants, one can certainly realise that there is an impressive continuity in the tradition, but without such a study one cannot understand or explain the complexity and diversity of the modern system of modes of Byzantine chant.

All these and other related investigations have given me a firm basis for my teaching of the present-day musical praxis.

*How has Byzantine chant changed over the centuries? How is it presently
sung in the liturgy?*

Byzantine chant has changed over the centuries through a number of
significant processes. The interplay and mutual influence of the oral
and written traditions is one. Some very well-known chants were
seldom if ever written down. On the other hand, the notated music of
model chants, such as the heirmoi or some 'stichera automela', served
only reference and learning purposes because singers had to know
their melodies by heart, as they had to adapt many other words to
them. As a result, all these chants were sensitive to change due to
inadequate memory, a sense of freedom during performance,
difficulties of adaptation, small changes in aesthetic standards, or
corrupt transmission. The oral forms of these chants was sometimes
written down, and it then became a written tradition subject to the
same use as the earlier one and so forth. This oral tradition could exert
at each time an influence on other written and more stable chants.
Through such processes, the music of the heirmoi appears changed
from the end of the thirteenth century onwards. Several local
traditions appear in the manuscripts in the fourteenth century, while
from the end of the sixteenth or beginning of the seventeenth
centuries we see the first record of the 'heirmologion' (book of the
heirmoi) under the name of one composer, Theophanis Karykis. By
the end of seventeenth century, we find the 'heirmologion' of Balasios
the Priest and in the second half of the eighteenth century, we find the
heirmologion of Petros Lampadarios, which is used today. All these
three heirmologia are records of the Constantinopolitan tradition
(with possible arrangements by their recorders), but we can assume
that they were widely disseminated due to the ever-growing role of
Constantinople as a national and musical centre during the Turkish
domination. Examining these heirmologia, one can follow the
continuity of the tradition and the course of changes. Another genre
of chants, the 'stichera idiomela' remained essentially unchanged up to
the seventeenth century. An embellished, but essentially old style,
form of the 'sticherarion' (book of stichera) appeared by the middle of
the seventeenth century. In the first half of the eighteenth century we
can imagine, or sometimes follow in manuscripts, a process of
simplification of the music of the stichera idiomela, with a parallel

influence of the music of the contemporary heirmoi on them. The final stage of this process was its written record by Petros Lampadarios (d. 1778). This is the so-called 'New sticherarion', which is sometimes sung today with minor changes or small embellishments

The method of reading notation is a second factor. As I have already mentioned, I believe I have proved that the notation was originally read 'at face value': one simple sign indicated one plain or sometimes slightly ornamented note. But we have also received two more ways of reading the old notation: short melismatic and long melismatic. These are, of course, part of our tradition and cannot be discarded. Given that, I believe that one can suppose that these changes in the conception of notation, from the syllabic to the long melismatic, occurred at certain points in time and this is exactly one of the fields of my investigations. Through such changes, chants became ever longer and this led to tendencies of more embellishment or, in the opposite direction, to simplification and abbreviations (cutting of some embellishments of melismatic chants). This is a very complicated story and cannot fully be described here. What is important is that changes in the music itself necessitated the development of the notation, and changes in the notation affected the music. The final stage of the notation, the reformed notation of the Three Teachers used nowadays, while capable of being fully analytical and describing every detail of the performance, has on the one hand facilitated the singing, but on the other hand has contributed to the deterioration of church music in the compositions of some modern composers through strong influences from the secular music.

A third point involves the tendency to more melismatic forms. I have already mentioned this with regard to the reading of the notation. But these tendencies can be traced in the compositions themselves irrespective of the way the notation is read. Melismatic chant seems to exist from time immemorial. However, a turning point in its history is the emergence of the so-called 'kalophonic' ('beautiful voiced', or embellished) chant in the thirteenth century and its subsequent development in the fourteenth and fifteenth centuries. A leading figure who also codified this chant is Ioannis Kukuzelis. This style was extremely melismatic, sometimes with inserted tropes, rearrangements of the text and very often meaningless syllables like 'terirem, to to, ti ti, ne ne na', etc. This style continued to flourish after the fall of Constantinople and has in fact left its imprint in the subsequent production of the whole Byzantine chant.

Finally, the transformation of intervals is an important factor to consider. In opposition to the views of many Greeks and, in the last decades, of some Western scholars, or to the present-day praxis where there is a plethora of musical intervals, I have good reasons to believe that Byzantine chant was originally diatonic with 'in principle' Pythagorean scales, the scales of the modes being exactly like those described by the ninth-century western musician Odo de Cluny. We know that the theory of the modes of the East was transmitted to the West. 'In principle' means that the relative position of the tonics of the modes is regulated by the intervals of the Pythagorean scale. As it concerns the intervals in the actual practice of singing the chants of a mode, I can notice that Pythagorean intervals cannot always be sung in a precise manner; the voice 'slips' frequently to slightly different intervals like those of mere intonation (instead of the Pythagorean major tone and 'leimma', i.e., small semitone, one sings a major tone, a minor tone and a big semitone). Although some acousticians also speak in favour of the contrary, I am sure that I observe such deviations in the present-day praxis for the case of modern modes with theoretically Pythagorean scales. In addition, this transition from a theoretically 'hard diatonic' (Pythagorean) to a 'soft diatonic' (using major and minor whole tones) can also be observed in the transcription of the Three Teachers, revealing a dual nature of the intervals, for some formulas at least (that is, one can sing these formulas either in hard or in soft diatonic).

All this makes me suspect that the original form of the scales is the hard diatonic transformed through musical praxis to the soft diatonic, which dominates the present-day praxis. Two modes, second and plagal second, went even further: they developed augmented seconds (intervals more or less larger then the whole tone) and became 'chromatic' ('chromatic' meaning exactly this in Byzantine chant). Again, such transitions from the hard or soft diatonic to the hard or soft chromatic (with larger or smaller augmented second respectively) can be traced in the present day praxis, in the transcriptions of the Three Teachers and in the manuscripts and the chants in their evolution over the centuries. The chromaticism in Byzantine chant has been a subject of great controversy. It was supposed by many western scholars that it constitutes an oriental influence. But, as I stated, it can with good evidence be seen as the result of a slow and continuous transformation in the system of Byzantine chant itself. On the other hand, one doesn't know the exact form of Arabic or Ottoman music of the medieval times to be able to speak about influence on Byzantine chant, although such influences can be suspected through the titles of some Byzantine compositions, such as 'Persian' and 'Tatarian'. In brief, I believe that the absence of instruments in worship, the absence of an exact theoretical description of the intervals, and the continuous musical praxis, contributed to the transformation of the intervals and the formation of the sound of the presently sung Byzantine chant, a sound not so much new but with a life of several centuries.

Most of the current repetoire of Byzantine chant consists of chants from the tradition of the eighteenth century, especially the records and compositions of Petros Lampadarios, which constitutes the tradition of the 'Great Church', i.e., the Church of the Patriarchate of Constantinople. Other older chants are, of course, sung, as well as later compositions, some of them following the tradition and retaining the ethos of church music, some of them slipping to secular styles. The same can also be said about the vocal style: traditional on the one hand, secularized (usually heavily and in a bad sense orientalised) on the other. Let's hope that research, teaching and, above all, true sense of the truth of the church will result in a better situation for this living tradition of a music, which has its roots – I'm happy to see this in my investigations – in the church fathers themselves.

How important is chant to Byzantine liturgy?
Chant has a central role in Byzantine liturgy. It seems that since the fourth century the chanted parts of the liturgy increased in number and, according to St Symeon, Bishop of Thessaloniki in the fourteenth century, describing the old cathedral, the so-called 'asmatic' (chanted) rite, everything in the liturgy was chanted in one or another way except the prayers of the priests. The cathedral rite declined after the Latin occupation of Byzantium in the thirteenth

century, in favour of the monastic rite, which was originally simpler but acquired many new hymns from the seventh/eighth centuries. These hymns were poetical and musical compositions of monks and church fathers such as St John of Damascus, St Kosmas the Melodist, and St Andrew of Crete. The rite became much more elaborated and chanted from the thirteenth century, incorporating the older melismatic chants of the cathedral rite while giving rise to the so-called 'kalophonic' chant referred to earlier. So, one cannot think of a service without chant today, although monks, hermits, or priests on ferial days, as well as individuals at home, can only read the services. This cannot hold true for the Divine Liturgy where the presence of at least one person except the priest is indispensable. At any rate, chant reinforces the meaning of the words and gives a further dimension beyond the mere understanding, not only to the words themselves but to the whole worship as well, approaching and reaching the 'kingdom of the heart' and the sense of the presence of the Lord.

Do you see any connection between Western chant and Byzantine chant?
This is a subject that I have not investigated but, as far as I know, one can see similarities and differences between them. To try to make a comparison, one must read the old Byzantine notation in the simple syllabic way and with the diatonic intervals I have described above. The long melismatic way of reading it is probably a somewhat later elaboration and obscures the immediate comparison. So, when one has in mind a 'face value' reading of the old Byzantine notation, one can discover many similarities, and some differences, between the Western and the Byzantine way of reciting the verses of the Psalms. One must of course compare the corresponding versions, i.e., compare a simple with a simple recitation and a melismatic with a melismatic. At least the simpler recitations bear similarities. I cannot at present say anything about the melismatic ones.

A very large portion of Byzantine chants consists of hymns. On the other hand, Western chant is based chiefly on the Psalms. So, one must again be careful about what is compared with what, although influences between different genres are not forbidden and should perhaps be investigated. There are some hymns (heirmoi or stichera) of Byzantine origin that were translated and entered the Western liturgy, and are used as antiphons, such as *Adorna thalamum tuum, O quando in crucem,* the antiphons for the Octave of Epiphany. The similarities of Western and Byzantine chant could maybe be more striking at the beginning. It is a field for investigation to reveal the details of these similarities and differences.

MUSIC AND CREATIVITY

Heidegger's Reading of Poetry: Art as Spiritual Exploration

Mark Patrick Hederman

THE DANGER AND THE DIFFICULTY with recent discussions on Heidegger as a man are the embargos they impose upon examination of his discoveries at the deepest level of human existence and his contribution to the history of philosophy. What could such a person have to teach any of us, and what could be the interest in a philosophy so tainted?

The burden of works such as *Heidegger et le Nazisme* (1987) by Victor Faria and *Martin Heidegger* (1991) by Hugo Ott, is to show that Heidegger was a paid-up member of the Nazi regime in Germany during the second World War and that his international standing and fulsome support gave credence to the doctrine of National Socialism, which might have been less plausible without such sponsorship.

I don't think it is possible to deny these ugly and disturbing facts. However, we still have to consider the possibility that even so vilified a philosopher could have made an important discovery and one that we would all be impoverished to ignore. Are we to close off a whole dimension of ourselves and declare it a no-go area because the person who discovered it is denounced as a reprobate? Should we deprive ourselves of penicillin because biographers discover its inventors to have been monsters?

My objection to books like Ott's biography is that they foist motivation upon Heidegger, without having had access to the archives of private papers that might verify such speculation. Alongside Ott's detailed and annotated presentation of the facts and events in Heidegger's life, there is a contextual commentary that situates these within an alleged psychological framework. Thus Heidegger's alliance with National Socialism and his bid to take control of university education in the Third Reich are interpreted as a lust for power. Heidegger hitched his chariot to the rising Hitlerite star so that he could become the educational giant of the Nazi pantheon. His repudiation of Husserl and removal of the latter's name from further editions of *Being and Time* (the original had been dedicated to Husserl) are attributed to professional jealousy or anti-semitism. His anti-Catholic behaviour, expressed in public utterances and private writings, are presented as unwarranted prejudices, at times biting the hand that fed him. He is said to have renounced the faith of his childhood and youth because it was a good career move. Nor was he slow to seek help from this Church when its influence might save him from later ostracisation.

Although the facts assembled by Ott to 'prove' his assumptions may be accurate and complete,[1] and I have no reason to discount any of them, I am not convinced by the way he uses these or by the conclusions he draws from them. I suggest that the following explanation of the same facts is at least as plausible.

Heidegger's alliance with National Socialism in Germany, far from being a sycophantic attempt to attach his career to its rising star, was rather an attempt to direct this movement and ensure its destinal purity by attaching it to his own. At least three Heidegger scholars would share this view: 'Heiddegger labored under the delusion that he could play the role of "philosopher king" to Hitler's *Fuehrersstaat* – which, to many, has suggested parallels with Plato's ill-fated venture with the tyrant Dionysius at Syracuse . . . Heidegger sought "den Fuehrer fuehren" (to lead the leader), Adolf Hitler, along the proper course so that the "National Revolution" might fulfill its appointed metaphysical destiny.'[2]

It was no petty political ambition that tempted him to flirt with this movement. His ambition was extravagantly more cosmic. He saw himself as one of those few people in world history whose name would survive as a household word when centuries had obliterated every military or political figure on the contemporary horizon. Heraclitus and Heidegger would make up two mountain peaks still visible when every other name in the twentieth century had been submerged in the valley of detail.

Otto Poeggeler tells us that 'already in 1933 Walter Eucken wrote that Heidegger feels himself to be "the sole and surpassing thinker since Heraclitus" and so "the born philosopher and spiritual leader of the new movement".'[3]

His weakness, as it seems to me, was neither greed nor ambition, but a creative infatuation that allowed him to project his own purposes onto the prevailing situation, imagining that his world-view coincided with the destiny of Germany. If he became the inspirational force behind all university education in Germany, he would fashion a whole generation in the light of his understanding of truth.

His promotion of the *Gleichschaltung* legislation, which entailed the transformation of university life in line with the Nazi *Fuehrerprinzip,* was not based upon political ambition or personal lust for power. It was based upon his conviction that he, and only he, was capable of guiding the universities along the path of truth, and that he was destined to do so. His own experience as a very gifted teacher, confirmed by anyone who knew him as such,[4] was that of being able to lead his students to a completely new way of living the truth. He believed that by multiplying this situation in as many universities as there were in Germany, he could both revolutionise the way of teaching and learning that characterised university education, and make that vital connection between the youth of Germany and genuine contact with Being, which would realign the Western world with its true destiny. In the winter of 1933–4, Carl Friedrich von Weisaecher could quote a Freiburg student: 'In the circle around Heidegger they have invented Freiburg National Socialism. Under their breath they say that the true Third Reich has not yet begun at all, that it is yet to arrive.'[5] Heidegger saw the Nazis as the heroic 'new barbarians' who would save the West from the dogmatic escapism of the Church, especially in its repressive attitudes towards so-called 'Modernism' on the one hand, and the inevitable decline that the culture of scientific technology must bring in its train on the other. National Socialism, under his guidance, could become the third way, and the 'destined' way between 'Bolshevism' and 'Americanism'.

This infatuation was shortlived. Both sides quickly realised that the other had a different agenda. And as soon as these fundamental differences became apparent, Heidegger became as arrogantly dismissive and courageously forthright as was his wont. Heidegger admitted that he had made a great blunder (*grosse Dummheit*) in aggrandising Hitler, but he regarded that as Hitler's fault and Hitler's business rather than any reflection upon his own thought or behaviour. In the famous interview given to *Der Spiegel,* he held that he had been betrayed by Hitler.[6] Heidegger's understanding of what should happen in Germany and in Europe once genuine contact had been re-established with Being, bore absolutely no resemblance to what was perpetrated by the Nazis and what constituted their political agenda. His opportunistic partnership with them even for a short time shows him to be culpably blind and politically naive, but it does not allow us to suppose that his philosophy was ever identifiable with theirs.

His objections to Husserl and to Roman Catholicism were not necessarily racial or religious. For Heidegger, the Judeo-Christian heritage was the cause of our present paralysis, our two-thousand-year-old amnesia. It was only through courageous apostasy that he was likely to escape from the tentacles of such institutionalised blindness. The Church's power over people was both historical and psychological. It was the source – and here was the ambiguity for Heidegger – both of the oblivion that it was his life's task to undelete and of his own extraordinary capacity to detect this, since it was the Church as his educator who had provided him with the wherewithal to undermine her. He had been trained by and through that very theology that had substituted itself for the reality it pretended to preserve. His education from early childhood had been undertaken and sustained, both financially and intellectually by the Church. The young philosopher would never have achieved the metaphysical stature that makes him one of the great thinkers of the century without the sustenance and discipline provided by the very institution that he later came to recognise as the Medusa he was destined to destroy. This was no petty rivalry, no small-minded vindictiveness: this was a fight to the death between contradictory opposites. There could be no pussyfooting or compromise with the arch opponent, that simulacrum of the truth, which was so near to it that it almost perfectly substituted for it.

This was David against Goliath, with the odds heavily stacked in favour of Goliath. The struggle was further complicated by an almost incestuous involvement between the two from Heidegger's earliest childhood. There must have remained a residue of bitterness in the young philosopher about the overweening and often prescriptive pedagogy of the totalitarian foster-parent. On at least three occasions his career as a recognised philosopher depended upon his openly declared allegiance to the philosophy proposed and maintained by the Roman Catholic Church. Such compromising preconditions to the only professional and financial advancement available to a young man from an impoverished background forced him to be ambiguous and later to be aggressively censorious.

The apparent rejection of Husserl was not necessarily because he was a Jew or for some motive of political expediency. It may have been his eventual realisation that his teacher's thought was comparatively superficial and the consequent danger that his own might be taken as a tributary to this, rather than as the uniquely revolutionary event that he came to believe it to be. Far from opening the way towards Being, Husserl was providing the older anachronistic ontology with a fashionable facelift that would allow it to reinvigorate itself and exercise further influence, when the real task was to reveal its obsolescence. Both Husserl and Jaspers were less original thinkers, but their popularity and reputation might obscure the real issues that needed to be addressed. Any identification of his own thought with theirs might excuse people from grappling with the full musculature of his originality. It was this scrupulous sense of responsibility that obliged Heidegger to dissociate his own thought from any other, especially those that might be deceptively similar. Any connection between the original philosophy of Heidegger and so-called contemporary philosophy (thus his refusal to be labelled an 'existentialist') would be a misleading decoy. Heidegger had to establish that he had no master and no peers in the realm of philosophical endeavour. If he had, he would have been grateful, and the first to recognise these. Neither Husserl nor Jaspers passed muster at this level, in his view.

All of which proves nothing and explains little. It is an attempt to waive the arguments that would suggest that Heidegger's thought should not be approached at all, that his behaviour exonerates us from any such effort. More than that, study of his work is retrospective collaboration with the Nazis. Needless to say, my view is that we should read him, that his thought is one of the liberating sources of philosophy.

Others claim that this thought is not just tainted by National Socialism because of a brief flirtation with that movement on the part of the author, but rather that this thought is the basis of that movement; it provides the philosophical backdrop to the historical aberration. Heidegger's metaphysics is the metaphysics of *Mein Kampf.* His philosophy is antisemitism in the depths of its being. Emmanuel Levinas, the great Jewish philosopher, is one of the most articulate exponents of this view.[7] Whereas some Christian theologians might claim that Heidegger's metaphysics is connected in some way to the God of Abraham, Isaac and Jacob, Levinas sees Heidegger as an atheist, whose philosophy is a religion in reverse. As a Jew, Levinas feels obliged to defend humanity against any piety afforded to mythical gods.[8] He commends Heidegger for pointing out the inhuman tendencies of technological science.

Heidegger returned to that moment of Western history where this technological option was first embarked upon. He condemns the philosophies that issued from the Socratic option. For this identification and discovery of the nature and the place of our departure along the road towards technology we owe him a great deal. But that is as far as we are prepared to go. We cannot and should not follow Heidegger in the arbitrary step backwards that he takes in trying to find the real meaning of life among the pre-Socratics. Levinas opposes such a step backwards in the direction of natural religion and even prefers the Socratic option to this idolatrous apostasy. He accuses Heidegger of trying to replace our forgetfulness of Being with a natural religion even more destructive and inhuman. 'Judaism denounces as idolatry . . . such sacramental powers of whatever kind, attributable to whatever divinity, which it sees as destructive of human freedom.'[9] Judaism in this regard is closely related to Socrates.

Heidegger's philosophy is much more dangerous than the technocratic option it condemns. Heidegger is proposing a religious enslavement to divine powers, a return to primitive religious thraldom. The essence of Judaism is to destroy the naturally religious tendencies of human beings and to inaugurate a stance that constitutes human freedom and enacts appropriate relationship between this world and the Divine. Levinas abhors the tendency of some contemporary philosophers of religion to return to pre-Socratic times to find in mythical prelogical language a privileged locus of contact between ourselves and the Gods. He claims that Jewish religious experience is discarded without a hearing while the most obscene and extravagant manifestations of primitive religious experience are paraded before us as the essence of intimacy with the divine. He even goes so far as to name the primitive religions that he abhors: 'The Sacred, he says, with all its fear and trembling – but also with the intoxication which its numinous presence inevitably excites – has become the key word and pivotal concept in a whole religious renewal. Whatever contemporary sociology can unearth in the prelogical mentalities of Australia and Africa are hailed as privileged religious experience.'[10] Levinas claims that it was precisely such natural religious instincts, such pagan idolatry, the most lethal of all our cultural instincts, that Judaism was called to destroy.

> Here you have the eternal seduction of paganism, right through to the infantilism of idolatry, which should have been surmounted definitively by now. Judaism is perhaps nothing more than the repudiation of that sacred, which filters through into the world. All this implantation within a countryside, this sacred attachment to place . . . in such a perspective technology is much less dangerous than the various household gods.[11]

Heidegger, taking a regressive step to circumvent the tyranny of technocracy, has founded another form of imperialistic tyranny far more odious: slavery to the truth of Being, which once again inflates the chosen subjects of manifest destiny to a state of unbridled freedom and uncontained development of self. Nor is this return to paganism a harmless eccentricity. It is the breeding ground for such political movements as National Socialism. For what else does such an understanding of Being produce other than the entirely selfish and situation-conscious growth of those trees called to make Being manifest. Nothing is to stop them or put them into question. They must establish their roots and grow as fully and as freely as possible. Their meaning, energy, source and goal is contained within themselves. Heidegger preaches unimpeded expansion in and from that place where the local tribe is called to manifest Being. Thus Heidegger's apparent atheistic sobriety is really an intoxicated paganism, an inverted religion. True religion, according to Levinas, is precisely what saves us from such gods.

Atheism is preferable to adoration of mythic gods. Judaism is the destruction of the numinous concept of the sacred and the rigorous affirmation of human independence. It puts God (and all gods) firmly back into their irretrievable otherness and prevents any possibility of infiltration of divinity into our world. Judaism exorcised the world and broke the spell of the enchanted forest forever. Any attempt to move back into such bondage and reinstate a natural connection between God and ourselves is retrograde and dehumanising. 'Myth, in however sublime a form, introduces into our souls a troubling element, that impure element of magic and witchcraft and that intoxication with the sacred which extends the animal in us into the civilised.'[12] Heidegger's God, for Levinas, is not too far away, but rather, much too close. He encroaches upon our hard-won freedom.

Once again, this position seems too simplistic, too trenchant, and it does not represent accurately enough Heidegger's attempt to pioneer a metaphysical passageway. 'The end of philosophy' for Heidegger is a place – but not a local or geographical one – a 'clearing' that makes way for the 'Other'. Heidegger's commentary on Holderlin and Rilke suggests two things: that there is a presence of the divine in nature, an infiltration, but that it is beyond 'thought'. Poetry is a way of human consciousness that reaches beyond the modality of thinking that is philosophical or scientific. But his work as commentator allows him to salvage for philosophy some of those realms 'beyond thinking' that stretch out before us when we reach that place where philosophy ends. The infiltration is not a power that invades and overwhelms our freedom, it is a sound that appeals to the sensitivity of those who have ears to hear with.

'Art is truth setting itself to work'.[13] The poet is 'like a passageway that destroys itself in the creative process for the work to emerge'.[14]

'By contrast, science is not an original happening of truth but always the cultivation of a domain of truth already opened'.[15] Something happens 'through' the poet that is contained in the work. This 'something' is the emergence of truth. 'All art, as the letting happen of the advent of the truth of what is, is, as such, essentially poetry'.[16] The poet engages in a kind of saying that is 'projective'. 'Projective saying is saying which, in preparing the sayable, simultaneously brings the unsayable as such into the world'. The function of the philosopher 'at the end of philosophy' is to embark upon another kind of thinking. This thinking will be repudiated by both the disciplines of philosophy proper and by literary criticism. It leads 'thinking into a dialogue with poetry, a dialogue that is of the history of Being' and which involves learning 'what is unspoken' by 'thinking our way soberly into what the poetry says'.[18] The objects of such attention are 'the traces of the fugitive gods'. These traces are not visible. 'Traces are often inconspicuous, and are always the legacy of a directive that is barely divined.'[19] But 'poets stay on the gods' tracks and so trace for their kindred mortals the way towards the turning'.[20] Turning is a kind of conversion, a new way of being human.

Heidegger recognises in Rainer Maria Rilke someone who has experienced the destitute times. He was a channel through which the 'song' emerged. Heidegger tells us that 'we are unprepared for the interpretation of the elegies and the sonnets, since the realm from which they speak, in its metaphysical constitution and unity, has not yet been sufficiently thought out in terms of the nature of metaphysics. . . . We barely know the nature of metaphysics and are not experienced travelers in the land of the saying of Being.'[21]

It is as if there are two ways of being in the world, one convex, the other concave. 'To put something before ourselves, propose it, in such a way that what has been proposed, having first been represented, determines all the modes of production in every respect, is a basic characteristic of the attitude which we know as willing.'[22]

Rilke is trying to change this kind of willing. This is what is meant by the 'turning', by conversion – another way of willing, another way of being. Rilke is calling for the establishment of a centre of gravity other than 'the physical gravitation of which we usually hear'. He calls it, therefore, 'the unheard of centre'. This marks the contrast between the two sources of energy described above. The second kind of person searches for the perfect physical centre through which to realise destiny in the order of humanity. The first kind is drawn towards a secret centre, which constitutes what Rilke refers to as 'the order of angels'. The earth has need of both these centres and of both these 'orders' to realise its survival, and to survive this realisation. Because it is not enough merely to subsist, we also need to accomplish existence. This happens if we are prepared to relinquish the 'covetous vision' of things, which we find natural, and adopt the 'double vision' which, when we juxtapose ourselves concentrically above the secret centre, allows us to see as 'a work of the heart' as much as of the eyes.

If you do reach the unheard-of centre, you can, through it, open yourself to the 'Open' and allow this 'breath' to spread up through you like a 'song' into the world. 'Song is existence', says Rilke. This is nothing like the impersonal fate that takes over the unwilling ecstatic and forces its way into our world. Nor is it the kind of political and ruthless 'will to power' that characterises 'will' in the normal sense of the word. This is 'singing' as 'poetry', as the unsayable coming through the words that the poet says, because the poet is turned towards another kind of hearing and living from the unheard-of centre. They are more venturesome, 'more daring by a breath', because they allow (freely will it so) something beyond their own consciousness to conspire with their saying and attach itself to their breath, so that the 'poem' is more than anything they ever could have done or said on their own, it is 'more daring by a breath' because it incorporates the unsayable from the unheard-of centre. In this way our earth becomes the possibility of being the world which we recapitulate, which we collect and give back again. Rilke spread himself fully to become the sound box for this 'organing impulse'.

Such presence of and to the 'Open' is described by both Rilke and Heidegger as a kind of 'turning'. 'In our having turned, there is implied a distinctive manner of conversion' says Heidegger, 'The distinctive feature of the conversion consists in our having seen unshieldedness as what is threatening us . . . It sees that unshieldedness as such threatens our nature with the loss of our belonging to the Open.'[23]

As well as our conversion, our self-emptying, 'turning' also implies 'that the Open itself must have turned toward us in a way that allows us to turn our unshieldedness towards it.'[24] Something from the outside touches us and 'when we are touched . . . the touch goes to our very nature and the will is shaken by the touch so that only now is the nature of willing made to appear and set in motion. Not until then do we will willingly.'[25] This last quote I find particularly important as an explanation of the meaning of 'will' for Heidegger, and also a key to the difference between the Heideggerian and the Nazi motivation. Will is the motivating force, the dominating energy in all our lives. The will to power is perhaps the mechanism of the universe as we find ourselves in it. But this is only because willing is the way we think we have to be, the way we crave to be because it is the motor-force that pushes us towards fulfilment. We are condemned to search for happiness, what we perceive to be the complete fulfilment of our being. Conversion occurs because we are stopped in our tracks, the tracks laid down by our habitual way of perceiving our destiny. Something 'touches' us and this is the beginning of our 'conversion', which is essentially a transformation of the nature and the movement of willing. All of which must occur in a place – although not a geographical one. Being 'rooted' for Heidegger is a mystical metaphor, we are talking about the 'inner domain of the heart' and 'the conversion of consciousness and that inside the sphere of consciousness'.[26] 'There, where the law touches us, there is the place within the widest orbit into which we can admit the converted unshieldedness into the whole of what is.'[27]

The mystery of the union of two wills is the kernel of the mystery of inspiration. 'In Wahrheit singen, ist ein andrer Hauch./ Ein Hauch um nichts. Ein Wehn im Gott. Ein Wind.'[28] (Really singing issues from a different breath. A breath from nowhere. A draft in God. A wind.) Something more has entered the work.

So, there is a space between, a difference between, Being and willing on the one hand – no foreign force invades and takes over my powers and faculties – but also between the two kinds of consciousness that such 'conversion' makes inevitable: 'The inner domain of the heart is not only more inward than the interior that belongs to calculating representation, and therefore more invisible; it also extends further than does the realm of merely producible objects.'[29] This is 'uncustomary consciousness', a new way of being conscious. 'Our customary consciousness lives on the tip of a pyramid whose base within us (and in a certain way beneath us) widens out so fully that the farther we find ourselves able to descend into it, the more generally we appear to be merged into those things that, independent of time and space, are given in our earthly, in the widest sense worldly, existence. True, this presence too, like that of the customary consciousness of calculating production, is a presence of immanence. But the interior of uncustomary consciousness remains the inner space in which everything is for us beyond the arithmetic of calculation and, free of such boundaries, can overflow into the unbounded whole of the Open.'[30]

If we pursue these paradoxical metaphors of boundaries overflowing and unbounded, we can follow Heidegger and Rilke to a place within ourselves that is 'heart' rather than 'mind', where 'existence beyond number wells up'. Here in 'the depth dimension of our inner being . . . this imaginary space . . . the widest orbit of being becomes present in the heart's inner space.' This is 'the innermost region of the interior'. Rilke is the poet of this dimension, but the philosopher is also necessary because 'Rilke gives no thought to the spatiality of the world's inner space; even less does he ask whether the world's inner space . . . is . . . grounded in a temporality whose essential time, together with essential space, forms the original unity of that time-space by which even Being itself presences.'[31] Whatever it is, Heidegger is aware that it is the most interior region that has ever yet been reached, and this can only increase the reality of humankind itself.

And this is where the philosopher is important and where a certain kind of critical endeavour is most helpful: In order to manifest 'the widest orbit of the open' through the most intimate interiority of the poet, Heidegger takes it upon himself to 'meet the poem halfway in thought' and to 'draw on other poems for help'.[32] The poet speaks from this innermost interiority and the poetry or what the poet says 'speaks not only from both realms, but from the oneness of the two, insofar as that oneness has already come to be as the saving unification'.[33] The order of the 'angels' is the unification of the two realms: 'The Angel is in being by virtue of the balanced oneness of the two realms within the world's inner space'.[34] The conversion of 'turning' is the transformation of our inmost interior into that 'equalizing of space', that spirit level that 'gives space to the wordly whole of the Open'.[35] It is a changeover 'from the work of the eyes to the work of the heart'.[36] The poet becomes a singer from the heart rather than a composer from the mind, and song is the breath from that inmost interior: 'Song is existence', which means that existence is that 'saying' between Being and ourselves, because 'in the song, the world's inner space concedes space within itself'.

From our side of this duet, in terms of human nature, this transformation is best accounted for in terms of will. The 'self-assertive' person is one who wills in the covetous fashion of the merchant, calculating from our perspective, the vision of things and the goal of all activity. Such willing is calculated towards productivity of the most useful and profitable kind. On the other hand, 'the more venturesome' or 'those who say in a greater degree, in the manner of the singer' are those 'whose singing is turned away from all purposeful self-assertion. It is not willing in the sense of desire. Their song does not solicit anything to be produced.'[37] And yet 'the more venturesome will more strongly in that they will in a different way from the purposeful self-assertion of the objectifying of the world. Their willing wills nothing of this kind. If willing remains mere self-assertion, they will nothing'.[38] Dimensions of interiority have been unearthed that supersede the comparatively superficial dimension within which subjectivity is the beginning and end of its own meaning and activity. The 'nothing' beyond the false self-sufficiency of humankind, which leads many theologians to the philosophical deduction of creation 'out of nothing', leads Heidegger to a further dimension, which is 'the track into the dark of the world's night'.[39] This dimension can never be recuperated for humanity by the covetousness of subjectivity. It is as though the 'heart' in our natural self-assertive order is concave, whereas in the 'order of angels' it becomes convex. The convex attitude of 'the heart' is a conversion of all the natural 'covetous' shapes and gestures into an attitude that 'accomplishes' rather than produces, 'a song whose sound does not cling to something that is eventually attained, but which has already shattered itself even in the sounding, so that there may occur only that which was sung itself.'[40]

Heidegger recognises that in the major poetry of Rilke 'only that which was sung itself' has occurred. This means that he is not entirely responsible for what has occurred, nor can he completely either name it or appropriate it. Heidegger is not a poet. He is a thinker. He must undertake the appropriate kind of literary criticism: 'Thinking is perhaps, after all, an unavoidable path, which refuses to be a path of salvation and brings no new wisdom . . . It has already renounced the claim to a binding doctrine and a valid cultural achievement or a deed of the spirit.'[41] These last two, the deed of the spirit, which becomes a cultural achievement, are the works of the poet. But they are not original to the poet, in a way that might allow the singer to either contain or control the origin of the song. A singer is one who allows the breath of existence to find its way through. It is a 'middle voice', whose reality is neither within nor without. Heidegger became a servant to this kind of song, at one remove from the singers themselves. His commentaries on Rilke are tentative and tremulous. The kind of literary criticism that can provide some exegesis for the song that is existence must be 'a step back from the thinking that merely represents – that is, explains – to the thinking that responds and recalls'.[42] He hopes, but does not 'know' that Rilke who is 'poetically on the track of that which, for him, must be said' is one of those 'sayers who more sayingly say . . . a saying other than the rest of human saying'.[43]

In fact, his final word about Rilke is in the conditional mood: 'If Rilke is a "poet in a destitute time" then only his poetry answers the question to what end he is a poet, whither his song is bound, where the poet belongs in the destiny of the world's night'.[44]

Heidegger is saying that we cannot afford not to read poetry, not to understand poetry, because poetry is our only detectable contact with Being. Our culture, according to Heidegger, has been founded on a lie, and Christianity, in some of its forms, has helped to promote and sustain that lie. And the lie is this: that it is possible to work out in our heads a logical system that will give us access to ultimate truth, to Being. The name of such a system is philosophy and the particular branch of that 'science' that deals with 'Being' and places it within our intellectual grasp is 'metaphysics'. Christianity borrowed that system, refined it and inserted into it the geometry of the God who had been revealed in Jesus Christ. Those who were very gifted intellectually and who had the time could master this intricate system and could become masters of metaphysics. They could then teach some very gifted disciples. The rest would acknowledge that the mystery was too deep for them, would be thankful that there were masters who actually did undertand the meaning of such intricate designs, would humbly accept crumbs of popularised penny catechisms, or would chew on jawbreaking terminology to eventually anaesthetise their curiosity.

Heidegger climbed to the top of this mountain and came back down to announce that there was nothing up there. The place was empty. His first work was designed to show that, and how, the history of philosophy had been one long self-induced amnesia. It is the story of the King's New Clothes told over twenty centuries. Not only had our culture lost all real contact with Being but they had substituted an alternative on the inside that was as convincing as the most intricate and true-to-life artificial flowers: the ones you have to smell and touch before you can tell that they are false.

The only real contact with Being, the only ontological language left in our culture is poetry of a certain kind. Not just any poetry. There are good poets and bad poets, there is poetry for decoration, for propaganda, for entertainment; there is poetry for lovers, for mourners, for magicians. But, according to Heidegger, there is also a metaphysical poetry: poetry that takes upon itself to give utterance to Being. Such utterance can only be done in words, can only be about the world around us. Our only access to Being is through the things and beings that surround us, even though none of those things is actually Being itself. Anything you can know or see is a 'being', a thing. These are all we have to work with. These include trees, dreams, mathematical formulae, music or hydroelectric dams. Nothing in this world is not a thing. A thing has its being but is not Being. Being is not any one of these things. Nor is it something hidden 'in' any of them. It is a no-thing. Nothing in our language, no word that we can invent, corresponds to 'Being' as such.

And yet, each one of us, from our earliest childhood, is aware of
'Being'; it is like the air we breathe, it is always at the back of our
minds. Metaphysical poetry, or 'great' poetry, opens our eyes to what
we have always already known. It makes us see what we were
insensitive to, what was always there but we had never adverted to. It
is a revelation of Being, an epiphany that shows us, in the ordinary
things and the everyday world that surrounds us, the transfiguring
and translucent light of the Being that energises them all, even while
it always remains invisible and absent from the palpable world we
graspingly inhabit.

The poet who says more is the one who dwells in that place
within, that is in contact with this reality, and so allows the breath of
Being to be caught on the sprocket of each word and thus secrete
itself into our culture as a luminosity or phosphorescence that coats
the poem as it emerges with its tang and its fragrance.

Great poets dwell in the secret places of the earth and their
essential heartwork is production of honey from these rocks. They are
what Rilke refers to as 'bees of the invisible'. Their poetry is language
drenched in the moisture of Being. The object of metaphysics is
never present, it is not there. Metaphysics has no object, in fact. So,
the process whereby we 'do' metaphysics – which is the 'doing' of
poetry – is one 'which at all times must achieve Being anew' as
Heidegger says.

But, whenever we have a sense experience, whenever we touch
something, smell something, hear something, see something, we
always and at the same time have a secret experience at another level.
There is always this delicate shimmering gossamer around every
experience that we, in our day-to-day commerce, our rush through
the business schedule, fail to notice and invariably ignore. This
second level experience of 'Being', which is not something added like
a coating or an undercarriage, but is something 'present' in its
reticent presentation of the thing to our notice, is something we have
to reactivate and examine. Almost as if we had to go back into the
dark-room of our experience and develop its implications from the
negatives of the day-to-day photo call. Because this second level
experience of 'Being' transcends our sense experience, we have to
invent nets that can collect this phosphorescence, entrap this

fragrance, filter this fine dust that always arises from our contact with reality, but which disperses and gets lost in the process of harvesting what we normally feed ourselves with. It is not the content of what we glean from this harvest that gives us access to Being, it is not the ideas we contain in our heads. It is the contact, the meeting with reality, that creates those sparks that we need to recover if we are to have any inkling of the real meaning, the ontological weight of those same experiences. This is what essential poetry tries to do.

Rilke describes this very beautifully to his wife Clara in a letter he wrote after he had seen the exhibition of Cezanne's paintings in Paris in 1907: 'Surely all art is the result of . . . having gone through an experience all the way to the end, where no one can go any further. The further one goes, the more private, the more personal, the more singular an experience becomes, and the thing one is making is, finally, the necessary, irrepressible, and, as nearly as possible, definitive utterance of this singularity . . . Therein lies the enormous aid the work of art brings to the life of the one who must make it, —: that it is his epitome; the knot in the rosary at which his life recites a prayer . . . for the utmost represents nothing other than that singularity in us which no one would or even should understand, and which must enter into the work as such, as our personal madness, so to speak, in order to find its justification in the work and reveal the law in it, like an inborn drawing that is invisible until it emerges in the transparency of the artistic.'[45]

But in order to really develop those negatives and invigorate the experience with absorbtive intelligence, a combination of critical thought and poetic transmission is recommended. This work engaged Heidegger in the last years of his life. He believed that unless we 'dwell poetically' on this earth, we are strangers here.

For Heidegger, the notion of 'poetry' and 'art' are almost interchangeable. In fact, they both describe that process that we invent to capture the evanescent reality that underpins everything and yet is unavailable to the categories of science or the language of ordinary discourse. Such 'art' or cunning is whatever form we can create that will capture the truth we are stalking, the essence of our obsession.

Notes

1.   'We now know that Heidegger's alliance with Nazism, far from being a temporary marriage of convenience, was grandiose and profound . . .' Richard Wolin, *The Heidegger Controversy* (MIT, 1993), p. 2.
2.   Richard Wolin, Hans-Georg Gadamer, Otto Poeggler cf. *The Heidegger Controversy*, ed. by Richard Wolin (MIT, 1993), p. 2.
3.   Otto Poegeller, 'Heidegger's Political Self-understanding', quoted in *The Heidegger Controversy*, ed. by Richard Wolin (MIT, 1993), p. 216.
4.   Cf. all the accounts, especially that of Hannah Arendt in Walter Biemel, *Martin Heidegger: An Illustrated Study* (London, 1977). Later revelations of the love affair between Heidegger and Hannah Arendt might cast some doubt on the objectivity of this particular testimony, but I do not see why it should. Cf. for example Ruediger Safranski, *Martin Heidegger, Between Good and Evil* (Harvard University Press, 1998) pp. 136–142.
5.   Quoted in Richard Wolin, op. cit., p. 205.
6.   Ernst Juenger in *Der Spiegel*, 18 August 1986, p. 167.
7.   I have elaborated this argument more scientifically and at greater length in an article called 'De l'interdiction a l'ecoute', *Heidegger et la Question de Dieu*, ed. by Richard Kearney and Joe O'Leary (Paris, 1980), pp. 285–295.
8.   Emmanuel Levinas, *Difficile Liberté* (Paris, 1963), p. 30. Translations from Levinas are my own.
9.   Ibid., p. 28.
10.   Ibid., p. 137.
11.   Ibid., p. 257.
12.   Ibid., p. 70
13.   Martin Heidegger, *Poetry Language and Thought* (New York, 1971), p. 40.
14.   Ibid., p. 40.
15.   Ibid., p. 62.
16.   Ibid., p. 72.
17.   Ibid., p. 74.
18.   Ibid., p. 96.
19.   Ibid., p. 94
20.   Ibid.
21.   Ibid., p. 98.
22.   Ibid., p. 110.
23.   Ibid., p. 122.
24.   Ibid., p. 122.
25.   Ibid., p. 125.
26.   Ibid., p. 127.
27.   Ibid., p. 126.

28. Rainer Maria Rilke, *The Sonnets to Orpheus*, 3. I have taken the German version from Stephen Mitchell's bilingual edition (New York, 1985), p. 22, but I have changed slightly his translation on p. 23.
29. Martin Heidegger, *Poetry, Language and Thought* (New York, 1971), p. 127.
30. Ibid. p. 128.
31. Ibid. p. 129.
32. Ibid. p. 131.
33. Ibid. p. 133.
34. Ibid. p. 135.
35. Ibid. p. 136.
36. Ibid. p. 138.
37. Ibid.
38. Ibid. p. 140.
39. Ibid. p. 141.
40. Ibid. p. 139.
41. Ibid. p. 185.
42. Ibid. p. 181.
43. Ibid. p. 140.
44. Ibid. p. 142.
45. *Rainer Maria Rilke: Letters on Cezanne,* ed. by Clara Rilke, (London: Vintage, 1991). Letter dated Monday, 24 June 1907, p. 4.

THE SINGING BODY:
MUSIC, SPIRIT AND CREATIVITY

Mícheál Ó Súilleabháin

AT THE HEART OF ALL HUMAN LIFE lies the spirit of creativity. *Homo Ludens* – man at play – manifests itself in the great and deep desire within each of us to create the very world we inhabit. As the very essence of things fall away before our every moment, our survival rests upon our ability to invest each living moment with a creativity born of the spirit. We reinvent ourselves, we conjure up creative myths and illusions, we – to paraphrase Heaney – sing ourselves to where the singing comes from.[1] On that stream of sound we exhale our life's breath even as we inhale the inspiration of the great beauty that lies secreted all around for us to find, for us to remain open to its revelation.

The writer George Eliot reminds us that at the heart of all human growth lies the element of choice.[2] It is the free choice of human play that lies at the heart of creativity. Choice is the essential edge that allows our breathing to cut through into a new reality. It is at the heart of the act of creativity itself. It is the blade that empowers our actions, and it is the ground that we build even as we build upon it.

How can we seek an understanding of this in the domain of music? In an article entitled 'Creative Process in Irish Traditional Dance Music', I explored this question within the context of one specific genre of music.[3] The element of choice was central to my findings. I suggested that there was a highly complex interactive pattern of choice-making in operation on several levels that was directly linked to the identity of the sound, and in this way linked also to the psychic identity of the music maker. My research suggested that the sonic fingerprint, so to speak, of the individual musician manifested itself through this element of choice within the very act of music performance itself. In this way Irish traditional musicians can recognise each other through the sounds they make. Also, a cluster of individual styles can identify a geographical region in terms of its collective patterns of traditional sounds. Thus, we speak of east Galway fiddling style, or Sligo flute style within that particular music tradition, or we speak of closed or open piping styles.

The intimacy of the choice-making is quite astonishing in its fineness. For example, the choice of up or down bow movements in fiddle music along with the choice of the number of notes covered in any particular sweep of the bow is one area of central importance. Add to this the minute improvisation in the selection of certain pitch patterns over others as 'allowed' within the shared aesthetic of Irish traditional music, and the improvised playing with rhythmic patterns within 'allowed' parameters, or the complex series of choices within the domain of 'phrasing' – how a musician chooses to group together the individual notes into segments – and what emerges is a wondrous tapestry of sound, invisible, untouchable, carried by patterned air disturbances from one human body to another, from the finger movements of the player to the drumming ears of a listener.

The living delicacy of musical intelligence seems to set it apart as far as its immediate sensitivity to the individual human spirit is concerned. The ability of music to sound out the vibrations of the individual soul, to create soundscapes of resonance sympathetic to the movements of the heart, to infiltrate the congealed valleys of the emotional body – all of these movements reflect the power of music to propel us onwards into the foreshadowed architecture of the sounds themselves.

Whenever I perform, I experience a sensation of 'going somewhere else' – an experience well documented in research of what might be termed either 'out of body', or 'into body' experiences of performers in action. What does this mean? The experience is one of allowing oneself to 'become the sound' itself, to move so closely into resonance with it that your central core is in fact the sound. The importance of body movement in this cannot be underestimated.

Gesture is at the heart of the sound-making process. A gesture, however slight, must be made before a sound can occur. The sound is therefore a sonic encodement of the body gesture – or more accurately, the interactive complex of body gestures – that created it. This encodement is transmitted though the sound into the body of the listener and has the potential to be retranslated back into a reconfigured variant of the complex of body gestures that created it. In this way the 'being in space' of one human may be transmitted to another.

Sometimes when I play privately the piano preludes of Chopin, I sense his presence not just in the sound but also in my body movements and posture. The irrepressible sadness of the B minor and the E minor Prelude in particular seem to me to be touch-sensitive to this finger-music of Chopin's torment. The calm despair of unrequited love that Hermann Hesse describes in his novel *Gertrude* seems to pervade this music.[4] Shades of the beloved George Sand seem to run and hide within the heaving and sighing of the B minor Prelude, and the very signature of lost love is mapped in the drooping semitones of the E minor Prelude. But this is not the music of despair. If it were, it would be silent. Instead it seems to me to encode the being-in-space of the pianist-composer's body as the thinking energy at the tips of his fingers runs like a shock back up his hands to lift the shoulders, cross the breast, and strike an arrow into his heart.

And what if we consider the player as listener to his own sounds? In this case the sonic encodements of the source gestures are multiplied in power and effect through a kind of psychic feedback. The sounds created through the finger patterns are carried to the performer's ear and serve to further inform the very finger movements that created them in the first place. This process is alive and constant where the level of concentration and sensitivity to this process is heightened through a multiplicity of factors – technical ability, mood, the music in question, the acoustics of the room, the presence of a certain audience, the light and shade in the room, the psychological history of the performer relative to the music being played, and many, many other factors. Then the optimum conditions are set for a form of transcendence that moves the performer into another place, into an altered windscape of the mind, where the creative process sings freely out through the body.

This is the sound of the body singing. And in spiritual terms it is the praising of God through a musical affirmation of being, no matter how tormented, no matter how joyous.

Music is not made though the mind – even if the mind is the cockpit of the endeavour. I often feel, as I watch my fingers move across the piano keyboard that I have ten brains, five on each hand, and an eleventh in my head, which informs and processes the others. But when the moment for take-off comes; for that moving into an altered state of being, I know that I must allow my finger-brains to take over and move into a kind of automatic state where my fingers are moved by something else. Is this the spirit coming though the singing body? Is this the quiet wind that heralds a Presence?

Music making then is a kind of 'throwing shapes' into the wind of inspiration. It is a conjuring act, a sleight of hand – above all it is a game. We might think of music as a kind of invisible lego-building in the air, a sonic game of encodement serving to construct invisible architecture for our souls to inhabit while the game is on. At its best, this is within the realm of angels. It is a coming home for our spirit, a moving into spiritual gear, a moving from the tempus of the world into the templum of the soul.

Music is a game of architecture in that it uses sounds to create form. Jung's description of the psyche is one that suggests a tension between structure and dynamic, in that he perceived it as a structure made for movement, growth, change, and transformation. He refers to these capacities of the human psyche as its distinguishing characteristics. When a musician improvises or plays creatively, he takes a given structure and rebuilds it in performance. It is the tension between that which is given and that which seeks to transform it through a creative flow. The opposition between stasis and flow, between structure and dynamic, between a given tune and the current of improvisation through it – these represent, to paraphrase Jung, the opposites that are the ineradicable and indispensable preconditions of all psychic life.[5] And it is out of this very tension that the singing body performs.

The singing body is the body in prayer. We are here in the domain of action. What the reflection of theology brings to prayer, that of musicology brings to music. Reflection may lead us towards a better and more successful singing and praying, but it still is not that which it reflects upon. The action of the singing body exists only in performance. It is a mystery of time, a timely spirit, a zeitgeist.

The dancing body is the singing body, and again the body in prayer. Gesture lies at the heart of all sound and all sound releases gesture. The dancing soul consumes itself in the vibrations of its own song, like Rilke's 'crystal cup':

> more gladly arise
> into the seamless life proclaimed in your song.
> Here in the realm of decline, among momentary days,
> be the crystal cup that shattered even as it rang.[6]

And it exists at T.S. Eliot's 'still point of the turning world' – that moment that is one of passive alertness – 'a white light still and moving'. It is the moment in Irish tradition when access is gained to the fairy fort (at the exact point of midnight, for example). It is also in that state of concentrated listening that we begin to hear the music within us – 'music heard so deeply/that it is not heard at all, but you are the music/While the music lasts'. And Eliot tells us where this point is, where the TimeSpirit dances. It is 'in the stillness/Between two waves of the sea', or it is 'At the source of the longest river'.[7]

The longest river in these islands is the Shannon, named after the goddess Sionna who sought out the secret and poetry and learning contained in the hazelnuts of wisdom. These she found on a hazel tree hanging over a deep pool. The ripe nuts were falling into the pool where they burst into bright purple colours and were eaten by the salmon of wisdom, which inhabited the pool. Sionna leaned forward, lost her balance and fell into the pool, which then rose up in anger at this disturbance and swept her into the sea. In this way the river Shannon got its name.

The search for the wisdom at the source of the river is the search for the river itself – just as in Kipling's novel *Kim*, the Llama searches out the river of the arrow, which sprang out of the ground where the Buddha's arrow struck. When he finally finds his beloved river, it lies within him waiting to be released through the floodtides of compassion.[8]

The river is found therefore through a precarious waiting on a time. Prayer is also precarious in that it too depends on a time. It demands a waiting, a sense of time, which music also demands. Coleridge writes:

> I warn all Inquirers into this hard point to wait – not only not to plunge forward before the Word is given to them, but not even to paw the ground with impatience. For in a deep stillness only can this truth be apprehended.[9]

And Kierkegaard reminds us that 'the impatient person therefore . . . makes demands in his prayers; the true man of prayer only listens'.[10]

The time of the river rests in its power to move and yet hold a still reflection. This is the still point where structure and dynamic meet. It is the still point of waiting for 'a music to occur', as Seamus Heaney puts it in *The Government of the Tongue*.[11]

Rational structure has been overtaken or gone through like a sound barrier. The poem does not disdain intellect, yet poetry having to do with feelings and emotions must not submit to the intellect's eagerness to foreclose. It must wait for a music to occur.

Prayer might be thought of as a kind of supersonic listening. What is received within the quieted mind in prayerful listening, 'Is a music that you never would have known/To listen for'.

> You are like a rich man entering Heaven
> Through the ear of a raindrop. Listen now again.
> (Heaney, 'The Rain Stick')[12]

Within the supersonic realm exists a music beyond our hearing. To reach upwards towards that music is to reach towards prophecy, like a praying mantis. A mantis is a species of insect that holds its forelegs in a position suggesting hands folded in prayer. The word comes from the Greek word meaning prophet. The poet within us, the musician, the dancer, the artist, reaches towards these prophetic realms by raising an eclectic antenna to capture signals out of the white noise 'between two waves of the sea'.[13]

> There may be in literature, music and the arts lineaments, spoors of a presentness prior to consciousness and to rationality as we know them. The analogy I have in mind would be that of 'background radiation', of 'background noise' in which astrophysicists and cosmologists see tracers leading towards, and vestiges of, the origins of our universe.
>
> George Steiner, *Real Presences* [14]

Our listening swims in the waves of sound, surfs the frequencies of air, and rehearses a heavenly order of things that exists in God's own time.

> In this way, the order of art becomes an achievement intimating a possible order beyond itself, although its relation to that further order remains promissory rather than obligatory. Art is not an inferior reflection of some ordained heavenly system but a rehearsal of it in earthly terms; art does not trace the given map of a better reality but improvises an inspired sketch of it.[15]

Wittgenstein speaks of 'the categories of felt being to which only silence or music gives access'.[16] This is where the silence of prayer meets the sound of music, where the emotion of 'felt being' carries us forward into the very space foreshadowed within the sound of silence. It is where music, spirit, and creativity find sustenance. It is home to the singing body.

Notes

1.   Seamus Heaney, *Open Ground, 1966–1996* (London: Faber and Faber, 1998)
2.   George Eliot, *The George Eliot Letters*, ed. by Gordon S. Haight (New Haven: Yale University Press, 1954)

3. Mícheál Ó Súilleabháin, 'The Creative Process in Irish Traditional Dance Music', in *Irish Musical Studies: Musicology in Ireland*, ed. by Gerard Gillen and Harry White (Dublin: Irish Academic Press, 1990).

4. Hermann Hesse, *Gertrude* (London: Penguin Books, 1963)

5. Andrew Samuels, Bani Shorter and Fred Plaut, *A Critical Dictionary of Jungian Analysis* (London and New York: Routledge and Kegan Paul, 1986)

6. Rainer Maria Rilke, *The Selected Poetry of Rainer Maria Rilke,* ed. and trans. by Stephen Mitcell, from the Orpheus Sonnets (New York: Vintage International, 1989)

7. T.S. Eliot, *Four Quartets* (Harcourt, Brace, 1974)

8. Rudyard Kipling, *Kim* (Oxford World Classics Paperback, 1998)

9. George Steiner, *Real Presences* (London: Penguin Classics, 1985)

10. Soren Kierkegaard, *Fear and Trembling* (London: Penguin Classics, 1985)

11. Seamus Heaney, *The Government of the Tongue: the 1986 T.S. Eliot memorial lectures and other critical writings* (London: Faber and Faber, 1988)

12. Seamus Heaney, *Open Ground*

13. T.S. Eliot, op. cit.

14. Steiner, op. cit.

15. Heaney, *The Government of the Tongue*

16. Steiner, op. cit.

MUSIC AND THEOLOGY

CHARLES TOURNEMIRE: A STUDY IN SPONTANEITY AND THE THEOLOGY OF THE CATHOLIC LITURGY

Cyprian Love

'WHEN YOU ASSEMBLE,' St Paul admonishes in his First Letter to the Corinthians, 'each one has a hymn, a lesson, a revelation, a tongue or an interpretation. Let all things be done for edification,' (1 Cor 14:26) for, as he later continues, 'God is not a God of confusion, but a God of peace' (1 Cor 14:33). 'Earnestly desire to prophesy,' he urges further on, '. . . but all things should be done decently and in order' (1 Cor 14:39–40). If we attempt to discuss the relationship between order and spontaneity in Christian worship, we are at once drawn back to the world of the New Testament letters as exemplified here. Here, the charismatic individualism of certain worshippers had to be coaxed into a productive and harmonious relationship with the external order required by corporate worship. Establishing a creative relationship between order and spontaneity seems to have been one of the earliest and fundamental issues in the Christian liturgical experience.

Paul finds an ally here in Jacques Derrida. For deconstructionists like Derrida, all identity is mediated through a sense of what it is not, so that identity involves the idea of difference and only at first sight conflicts with it. Difference makes identity possible: difference is admitted to the idea of sameness. Thus, for Derrida, there is a dismantling to be done of unreal antitheses in which one element is privileged, such as in the supposed modern Western priorities of reason over imagination, analysis over intuition, rationality over mysticism, and so on:

> We could . . . take up all the coupled oppositions on which philosophy is constructed, and from which our language lives,

not in order to see opposition vanish but to see the emergence
of a necessity such that one of the terms appears as the
differance [i.e., *différance*] of the other, the other as 'differed'
within the systematic ordering of the same (e.g., the intelligible
as differing from the sensible, as sensible differed; the concept
as differed-differing intuition, life as differing-differed matter;
mind as differing-differed life; culture as differed-differing
nature; and all these terms designating what is other than
physis – techne, nomos, society, freedom, history, spirit, etc. –
as physis differed or physis differing: physis in differance).[1]

If the identity of a liturgical form is first taken to be its received
structural order, then on Derrida's premises, let us now 'earnestly
desire to prophesy,' because this liturgical order needs spontaneity to
complete it. They constitute a conversation between equals:
spontaneity as 'differed-differing' structure.

A noteworthy tradition of liturgical spontaneity was exhibited in
the Roman Catholic Church earlier in the twentieth century by a
celebrated succession of organists at some larger churches in France,
which contributed to a national culture of organ improvisation. It is
true that the eighteenth-century German Lutheran Church, which
produced J.S. Bach, had a great tradition in this sphere; likewise, the
French Catholic Church of the same period had its improvisatory
genius in men like Couperin. Nevertheless, organs and organists at
this earlier period were rarer and more exotic, and the impact of these
improvisatory schools at a popular level could hardly have amounted
to a significant contribution to pastoral liturgy. By contrast, the late-
Romantic and post-Romantic school of musical improvisation we are
discussing was a widely recognised and internationally respected
French institution. Charles Tournemire, arguably the greatest
improviser of this tradition, will be considered here especially, and in
both a musical and a liturgical light. A liturgical light, because he
upheld to a level of genius a vital spontaneity in the liturgy through
his art of improvising, an art that did not tug against the received
liturgical structure, but grew out of it, in a delicate equipoise of
freedom and rootedness. He declared his art to be 'very narrowly
circumscribed by the liturgy[2] and he shows how to be spontaneous in

the liturgy, but at the same time how such spontaneity may be thoroughly respectful of the existing form of liturgy. At a practical level, this liturgical rootedness arises from his ideological preference for Gregorian chant, the official and ancient music of the Roman Rite, as the thematic basis of his improvising, and in improvising on Gregorian melodies he restored to them in a certain sense what is their own, for it is widely believed by writers in the field of medieval musicology such as Leo Treitler, David Hiley and Peter Jeffery[3] that spontaneous improvisation by liturgical cantors contributed to the growth of this chant in the Middle Ages. (The parallel between Tournemire's improvisation and medieval practice is not exact. Tournemire's is creative improvisation in the sense of poesis, whereas medieval chant improvisation seems to have had more to do with preserving chants being passed down in an oral culture. Its 'object and effect is to preserve traditions, not play loose with them'.)[4] The musical freedoms that Tournemire displayed anticipated, in the period between the wars, a recovery of the New Testament liturgical spontaneity with which Roman Catholics are familiar since the Second Vatican Council. It is important to acknowledge the prophetic role of organ music in this instance, for it is more often seen as linked to a conservative liturgical style, rather than as a foretaste of things to come. Can any liturgist show, from the same period, freedoms in relation to preaching, participation or style of celebrating the liturgy comparable to those exhibited by musicians like Tournemire in the improvisatory tradition? It is interesting to notice that, just as improvisation has always been regarded as a special strength of French musicians, it was largely from French theology that the impetus for the Catholic Liturgical Movement in the 1950s chiefly came.

This Liturgical Movement in the 1950s paved the way for Vatican II. Since that Council, we recognise that liturgy is more than an activity 'done *to*' the worshipper, it is something 'done *by*' him or her. Sacred time is not just time spent, and it must be explored in terms of its artistic possibilities. This exploration implies a spontaneous dimension, for if the liturgy is to accommodate itself to the human person it has to recognise that humans are by nature heuristic, discoverers of their environment and its potential. Because human nature is an embodied nature, humans participate liturgically as embodied, and their spontaneity may be expressed outwardly. To resist this corollary is to cling to a Cartesian dualist anthropology of mind and body. Liturgical spontaneity does not mean simply thinking spontaneous thoughts or praying spontaneous prayers interiorly. Humans are not pure spirit, and their spontaneity is fully that of the whole embodied self in freedom visible, freedom shared with the liturgical community in word, act and symbol.

Tournemire's art was rooted in Gregorian chant, which was seen by him as the bridge between organ and liturgy. An awakening of interest in Gregorian chant was already underway in the period of Tournemire's early life. The monks of Solesmes had been exhaustively researching the origins of chant, and the Schola Cantorum was founded in 1894 for the study of early music. In 1904, Pope Pius X sanctioned the preparation of an official edition of chants, the *Editio Vaticana*. Charles Widor, one of the great organists and improvisers of the period and a one time teacher of Tournemire at the Paris Conservatoire, had an audience with Pius X, who said: 'What is my wish? To separate the music of the Church from the music of the theatre, and put a little order into the ecclesiastical chant.'[5] This remark about the theatre is significant as a barometer of Church music-making at that time. Organists from the nineteenth century on, including the greatest such as César Franck, were quite happy to include, in their usual performances in church, solo pieces that, while they might make a magnificent and emotional contribution to the liturgy, and even possess a mystical feel, were not in any declared or exclusive sense religious music and were not at all out of place in the concert hall. Such music might come to be seen as chiefly liturgical, partly by association and because it was for the organ, but it did not grow out of the liturgy as such. It might be religious emotion, but it was not liturgy, nor was it usually linked to the chant thematically. This is a factual statement: it is not an arbitrary judgement, and, in fact, such music can well be seen as announcing a certain interaction between liturgical and secular reality, a kind of meeting point of church and world, in an entirely constructive and indeed rather modern sense, especially placed before or after the service as it usually was, in the form of a prelude or postlude. The position of organs above the west door of French churches effectively enhanced this 'transitional' aesthetic. In fact, some of César Franck's greatest organ pieces, the *Three Chorales*, are built upon fictitious chorales or hymn-tunes, in a kind of imaginative, romantic gesture towards the idea of objective liturgical reference. Charles Widor's great organ *Symphonies*, the *Gothique* and *Romaine*, are based on the Easter and Christmas chants 'Haec Dies' and 'Puer Natus'. Nevertheless, most of their music, and that of comparable composers, does double duty in church and concert hall, and does it very well. This point serves to throw into relief the essential nature of Tournemire's art, for the devotional style of both his improvising and his compositions, particularly *L'Orgue Mystique*, is like a fish out of water in the concert hall, in much the same way as stained glass does not sit comfortably in an art gallery. Like stained glass, they take their meaning from an all-embracing liturgical sensibility.

Having sketched the liturgical issues raised by this French school of organ improvising, it is time to look at Tournemire from a more particularly musical point of view. Firstly, he needs to be listened to with an ear for the underlying chant so skilfully used, the exquisite balance between derivation from the chant, and flamboyant creativity. As Tournemire's pupil, Maurice Duruflé, expresses it in the preface to his painstaking transcriptions from recordings of Tournemire's improvising:

> The soaring of his imagination was at once poetic, picturesque, capricious, then at a turn impassioned, tumultuous, abandoned, then suddenly again, blandishing, mystical, ecstatic. The Gregorian chant book was ever before his eyes in the organ desk, and he sought his inspiration exclusively in liturgical themes impregnated with the most spiritual sentiments. The fortunate hearers who saw or heard this prodigious man will never forget the emotions they owed to him.[6]

It might be appropriate at this point to consider the broad nature of improvisation. Certainly it is the most primitive form of music that can be produced. Humans must first discover, or improvise, music before they can attempt to fix it in permanent form. Improvisation must have come first in the musicality of prehistoric human persons. Perhaps it still remains the primordial musicality of the person: it has been noted that '. . . most people produce music by themselves for one or two hours a day, mainly by varying what they know or combining the known tunes according their tastes.' Ethnomusicologist Bernard Lortat-Jacob asked fourteen contributors to his collection *L'Improvisation dans les musiques de tradition orale* to provide him with a short definition of improvisation.[8] From the highly diverse responses, certain phrases tend to emerge: improvisation is composition in real time; it is the desire for unique and unpredictable utterance; composition in movement rather than repose; spontaneity. For one writer, improvisation is where music becomes most fully human, because human behaviour is spontaneous. Nevertheless, it is understood that all improvisations are rooted in some kind of pre-existent model. This will either be the wider model implied by the stylistic horizon that the improviser adopts automatically as a result of his own musical culture, as when a European improviser improvises to sound like Western art music or folk music. Or it will be a wider cultural musical model that the improviser more or less consciously assumes, as when a European improvises so as to sound like Oriental or African music. Or again it may involve a model consisting of more specific pre-existent material, very often a pre-existent tune or motif. According to one contributor to the Lortat-Jacob symposium, the traditional improvisation of primary oral cultures, those cultures with no form of literacy, consists entirely of this last type, that which is based on pre-existent motivic material.

Even if the last claim seems sweeping, it remains the case that for musical improvisation in primary oral culture, there is at least a tendency to base the improvisations on some kind of repeated pre-existing formulae, and in this respect the improvisation of music is comparable with the idea of improvisation in epic poetry. Milman Parry and Albert Lord[9] revolutionised the study of Homer by pointing out that the *Odyssey* and *Iliad* were heavily dependent upon the repetition of such regular formulae, essentially the ossified residue of ancient bardic techniques of memorisation. Moreover it might be said that, even when an improvisation seeks to be free of dependence upon pre-existing material, it tends to generate its own repeating motifs from within with a view to attaining cohesion. Thus an improvisation in this latter sense frequently improvises on itself, and aspires to cohesion by adapting some particular fragment of itself. In either case it seems that improvisation seeks a form of inner cohesion by returning to some recurring fragment.

At this point we start to draw out the theological implications of Tournemire's spontaneity in the liturgy. For Christian theology, in the whole of created being there is no such thing as neutrality. Created being does not sit statically apart from God but is made to be drawn back to Him and up to Him in its innermost nature. The Christian liturgy is therefore a journey back to God, and a shadow and foretaste of the Heavenly Liturgy. It is fitting that a characteristically liturgical form of music should be evanescent, not like permanent composition, and should share in the liturgical movement of becoming-into-God, wholly wedded to the liturgical moment that produces it, so that liturgy and music both slip into the past together as the liturgy journeys on. In this way, music is not perpetuated in what would here be a false present. Improvisation is a reverie built around a liturgical moment. If we cling to it to possess it, we forget that in the liturgy it is God who possesses mankind in history, not mankind that possesses Him in its own present. Liturgy for the Catholic tradition, as expounded, for example, in the encyclical *Mediator Dei* of Pope Pius XII, is the fullness of the Divine action in history, a historical becoming in the hand of God, not a static being in the hand of man. Musical improvisation, considered as evanescent, is consequently a particularly apt expression of liturgy.

Now that we have touched upon the dynamic becoming in which all liturgical reality consists, it can be seen that Tournemire's improvisation, taking Gregorian motifs from the liturgy and transforming the hearers' perception of them by subjecting them to an imaginative process, freed the hearers for a form of self-transcendence within the liturgical framework. The imaginative musical reverie of his and all similar improvising constantly recreates liturgical reality for the hearers by recreating the existing gregorian material of the liturgy, and in this way humanity's most salient attribute of freedom is enshrined within the liturgy, at the very place, that is, where humanity is fully swept up into becoming. Creative imagination is here not sequestered from reality according to a model that sees the 'real' and the 'imaginary' as polar opposites. It is a communication whereby we pass beyond ourselves to connect with the real other, emergent reality. The improviser, operating out of the open-endedness of imagination, is particularly close to the idea of reality considered as emergence and becoming. In this he has a proper role in penetrating the inner movement of liturgy and sharing that penetrative insight with others. In the words of Gaston Bachelard 'imagination separates us from the past as well as from reality; it faces the future. To the function of reality . . . should be added the function of irreality which is equally positive . . . If we cannot imagine we cannot foresee . . . the function of the real and the function of the irreal must be made to co-operate.'[10] For Ray Hart, the 'ontological reach' of the imagination refers to the order upon which it opens and in which it participates. Imagination intends, and extends, the realm of the 'coming to be'. Stated abstractly, the domain upon which imagination opens is ontological incompleteness, being aborning . . .'[11]

Since Kant argued that time was not an objectifiable concept but a 'form of intuition,' something within which thought takes place rather than an object of thought itself, we have become accustomed to the idea that time cannot be referred to univocally. Time is often referred to metaphorically, and in theology, notions of sacred history 'flowing', and eschatology 'beckoning' all participate in this language of imagination. Tournemire is referring to time in a parallel way. It has been seen how Tournemire's genius involved a commitment to what is given concretely in the liturgical text, and how he then surpasses the latter into the emergent world of the imagination. Tournemire's improvisation is literally *sur-real*, built upon reality but also transcending it, so that his imagination surpasses the real to a new expression of reality as becoming. When we reflect with him on the liturgical chant, we reflect on it under the aspect of possibility and face the future. In parallel fashion the liturgy itself attempts to fix our minds not on what is physically there, but on what we must imagine, the heavenly liturgy, of which what we see physically is only a reflection. Tournemire's imaginative departure from the chant is therefore neither a departure from the liturgy, nor a distraction from it, nor even distortion, or decoration. Like all true liturgical spontaneity, it is in fact a form of knowing, knowing that may, as here, to borrow words of Roger Scruton, touch the heart but numb the tongue.[12] Spontaneous imagining in outward expression within liturgy metaphorically captures our experience of futurity and is a primitive sign of hope. Semiologically, it gives rise to a sign where the signifier is spontaneity and the signified is futurity. Within the specific limits of liturgy considered as the major text of Christian cultural discourse, this sign carries an encoded statement about the Christian's relationship to eschatology. It is not absolutely essential to the implementation of this dynamic that the improviser improvises on a pre-existent musical motif taken from the received text of the liturgy. Where the improviser refrains from doing this and improvises freely without conscious dependence on a particular musical fragment or fragments from the liturgy, he or she improvises on the *whole liturgy* conceived as unified motif simply because he or she is improvising in that place at that time.

In short, imagination and liturgy both *look forward.* Of conscious imaginative acts spontaneity is the purest because in spontaneity the mind seeks to minimise dependence on its past: spontaneous art is, ultimately, improvisatory art. Improvisatory liturgical art will speak of the goal of being, where Christ will be all in all in the Heavenly Jerusalem. Improvisation is an intuitive insight into ultimate transcendence, a non-verbal pointer to, rather than an explaining of the liturgical community's goal. The involvement of musical experience in the arena of rational meaning, a semantic of aesthetic experience, 'how it is that we perceive qualities in things – paintings, books, melodies, plays, – that we do not feel we can assert literally to be there'[13] – is one of the major motifs of aesthetic theory. Tournemire opens up a neglected channel of liturgical sensibility, therefore, so that the liturgy's journeyhood, dynamic return to God, its nature as becoming, are brought into relief – brought into relief by analogy with the emergent nature of spontaneous aesthetic imagining, which, finding a foothold in the gregorian text, draws liturgical insight with it as it soars aloft. Improvisatory liturgical music has, it seems, been socially constructed here by the liturgical community as a metaphor for the hopeful way the Christian life is lived. To borrow the words of John Shepherd, music has here invoked 'the immanent social structures through which people, events and objects are held in particular relationships with one another',[14] in this case a shared hope in an eschatological society:

> Musical meaning is not ultimately a 'thing apart,' different in some unexplained way from all other kinds of meaning. If language refers disjunctively and cognitively to the visually separable people, events, and objects through which social structures are given life, then music may invoke conjunctively and corporeally the immanent social structures through which people, events and objects are held in particular relationships with one another. It is the same world that is being mediated and constituted symbolically.[15]

This link between musical improvisation and hope is, I suggest, a mark of that other highly significant improvisatory musical tradition of the twentieth-century West – jazz – and the comparison is helpful at this point. Jazz had first arisen within an oppressed black community in which hope for an emancipated future was a deeply inscribed social image, no less than it is within Christianity with its hope for the afterlife. Jazz improvisation, no less than the liturgical improvising, serves to 'constitute sets of collective images which motivate a society towards a certain mode of thinking and acting'.[16] In the words of Ricoeur: '[I]magination works in two different ways. On the one hand, imagination may function to preserve an order. In this case the function of the imagination is to stage a process of identification that mirrors the order. Imagination has the appearance here of a picture. On the other hand, though, imagination may have a disruptive function; it may work as a breakthrough. Its image in this case is productive, an imagining of something else, the elsewhere.'[17] In the case of jazz, and Tournemire's liturgical improvising, there is just this imaginative preserving and mirroring of an existing social order in the form of tunes improvised upon. The improvisation arising from this pre-existent material then effects the 'breakthrough' and imagination of 'the elsewhere'. Musical improvisation shows the liturgical community that its past has a future. 'I looked, and behold in heaven an open door.'

Notes

1. Jacques Derrida, 'Différance', in *Speech and Phenomena and Other Essays on Husserl's Theory of Signs* (Evanston: Northwestern University Press, 1973), pp. 148–149.

2. Norbert Dufourcq, 'Visites diffusées des églises Saint Sulpice, Saint Eustache, Ste Clotilde et Notre Dame de Paris', *Les Amis de l'Orgue,* numéro special (1936), 21.

3. See for example Peter Jeffery, *Re-Envisioning Past Musical Cultures: Ethnomusicology in the Study of Gregorian Chant* (Chicago and London: Chicago University Press, 1992).

4. Leo Treitler, 'Homer and Gregory: The Transmission of Epic Poetry and Plainchant', *The Musical Quarterly,* 60, no. 3 (1974), 333–372, (p. 346).

5. Charles Widor, *Initiation Musicale* (Paris, 1923), p. 107. Cited in Andrew Thomson, *The Life and Times of Charles-Marie Widor 1844–1937* (Oxford: Oxford University Press, 1987), p. 68.

6. Maurice Duruflé, preface to Charles Tournemire, *Cinq Improvisation pour orgue reconstituées par Maurice Duruflé* (Paris: Durand, 1958), p. ii.

7. Mária Sági and Iván Vitányi, 'Experimental Research into Musical Generative Ability', in *Generative Processes in Music: The Psychology of Performance, Improvisation, and Composition,* ed. by John Sloboda, (Oxford: Clarendon, 1988), p. 186.

8. See Bernard Lortat-Jacob, 'Improvisation: quatorze définitions' *L'Improvisation dans les musiques de tradition orale,* ed. by Bernard Lortat-Jacob (Paris: SELAF, 1987), pp. 67–70.

9. See for example A.B. Lord, *The Singer of Tales* (1960) (New York: Atheneum, 1968).

10. Gaston Bachelard, *The Poetics of Space* (1958) (Boston: Beacon Press, 1964), p. xxxiv.

11. Ray Hart, *Unfinished Man and the Imagination: Towards and Ontology and a Rhetoric of Revelation* (1968) (Atlanta: Scholars Press, 1985), p. 135.

12. See Roger Scruton, *The Aesthetics of Music* (Oxford: Clarendon, 1997), p. 132.

13. Clifford Geertz, 'Notes on the Balinese Cockfight', in *The Interpretation of Cultures: Selected Essays by Clifford Geertz* (New York: Basic Books, 1973), p. 444.

14. John Shepherd, 'Music as Cultural Text', in *Companion to Contemporary Musical Thought,* ed. by. John Paynter, Tim Howell, Richard Orton and Peter Seymour, (London: Routledge, 1992), I, p. 153.

15. Ibid.

16. Richard Kearney, *Poetics of Imagining from Husserl to Lyotard* (London: Harper Collins, 1991), p. 157.

17. Paul Ricoeur, *Lectures on Ideology and Utopia,* ed. by George H. Taylor, (New York: Columbia University Press, 1986), pp. 265–266.

Church Music and the Reformation

Fintan Lyons

Introduction

The Reformation, begun in 1517 by Martin Luther's protest against indulgences, was a watershed event in the life of Europe. The streams of religious, social, cultural and intellectual life met, combined, took new directions, and affected each other in new ways. In music, the effects of the Reformation were not confined to worship in church but were to be felt in musical culture generally – in public entertainment, for example, in domestic leisure activity and even in the ballads sung in the streets.

From another perspective, of course, music can be seen to have its own history, and then the Reformation is one factor in its evolution. The Reformation in religion occurred in a Europe already experiencing profound change, social and political, cultural and intellectual. Of particular importance was the invention of printing, which facilitated the spread of a new intellectual movement, humanism, with its critical spirit and re-discovery of classical culture. The individual emerged on the scene in a way that had not been possible in earlier centuries when social and religious conditions imposed a greater sense of the collective, and self-expression was limited to the few. Italy led the way in this re-birth, or Renaissance, and while it contributed many artists to the creation of a new culture, it attracted many from other countries as well, and particularly in music. Among them was the composer, Josquin des Prés (d. 1521), whom Luther was greatly to admire. He and other composers, whether in the papal court or those of the nobles, composed many masses, but their output reflected too the culture of the age in the great number of *chansons* required for secular occasions. Music, both ecclesiastical and secular, was an expression of the culture of the time.

This culture was shaken to its medieval foundations by the Reformation. Much was changed and yet there was also a continuity: 'nearly everybody in the West before the Reformation, and probably most people after it, were traditional Christians'.[1] For a generation, change was most obvious within the narrow confines of worship, and social life continued to be determined by the secular authority – the royalty in England, the princes in Germany, the town councils in Switzerland. The evolution of musical culture before and after the Reformation is bound up with the emergence of new social categories, as the bourgeoisie availed of improved economic conditions to develop cultural interests. Not all the characteristics of the music found in the Reformation churches are then due to the new theology but can be seen also as part of music's own development in a changing society. Overall, the relation between music and the Reformation is quite complex, so in this brief study the relatively simple course will be followed of describing how music used in worship was affected by the theology and spirituality of the Reformation. It will also emerge that this process went beyond the area of church music to create new forms of musical culture in the social sphere.

The Reformation in its diversity

The main church traditions arising directly from the Reformation can be grouped into Lutheran, Reformed and Anglican, according to the theological and liturgical inheritance received from the principal Reformers. In reaction to the Reformation itself a more radical movement gave rise to its own church traditions, generically described as Anabaptist and diversified subsequently into Mennonite, Moravian and other groups characterised by adult baptism and socially separatist tendencies. Baptist churches derive mainly from the Puritan tradition, established by those in the English Reformation influenced strongly by Swiss Reformed theology. From eighteenth-century Anglicanism there arose a revivalist movement, which became in time a worldwide church, Methodism. All of the foregoing trace their theological and liturgical traditions back to the Reformation and are generally referred to as Protestant churches, though Anglican churches generally prefer the description Catholic and Reformed, because of theological differences between the English and the Continental Reformation.

It can be said that the various Reformation traditions developed distinctive patterns of music in their worship, though a certain communality remains because of basic similarities between the liturgical rites adopted by them. This was so because some principles affecting worship, and therefore music, were held in common by the Reformers. The basic idea to which they all appealed when introducing changes in the form of worship was the need to establish new patterns in accordance with the theological principles of the movement. There was a need to eliminate various rituals that were contrary to the new theological understanding or no longer understood by the people. This was described as purifying worship of superstitions. It was considered vital also to enable people to participate more fully in worship through the use of the vernacular, through the more extensive use of scripture, and through lessening the distinction between clerical and lay involvement. The implications of this policy for church music resulted in an increase in some ways of its role and a reduction in others.

Lutheranism
Martin Luther (1483–1546) is considered the father-figure of the Reformation, though two unorthodox groups in the fourteenth and fifteenth centuries, the Lollards in England and the Hussites in Bohemia, are regarded as forerunners of his movement. Luther was of a conservative mind in matters liturgical – he was in fact shocked at the changes introduced into the Mass by his own followers, including the introduction of the vernacular, during his absence from the town of Wittenberg in 1521. This regard for tradition had an important bearing on the form taken by the liturgical changes he introduced, including the musical elements of the liturgy. Compared with the changes introduced by the other major Reformers, Luther's liturgy retained more of the elements, both recited and sung, of the medieval mass.

Nevertheless, his theological position led him to make significant changes. As he denied the mass was a propitiatory sacrifice, the offertory (and the music provided for it), which appeared to have

strongly sacrificial language, was suppressed in his first edition of the
new liturgy, the *Formula Missae* of 1523. The Canon of the mass was
greatly reduced and communion administered in both kinds. His
conservatism prevented him from making some changes at this stage
that his theological principles would have called for. For example, he
considered that all liturgy was in essence a celebration of the Word,
the mass being in essence the recitation of Christ's last will and
testament, contained in the Narrative of Institution ('Take this all of
you . . .'). Consequently, it was of vital importance that the people
should hear these words. Luther made a gesture towards this by
requiring them to be chanted aloud rather than in a whisper as the
rubrics indicated. But in 1523 they remained in Latin, as did the
whole of the celebration, apart from the reading of the epistle and the
gospel. This meant, however, that much of the old Latin music could
be retained. So the Introit, Kyrie, Gloria, Gradual, Alleluia, Sanctus,
Benedictus, Agnus Dei (this last during the distribution of
communion) continued to be sung by a small choir, a *schola*. In the
introduction to the rite, he says that these chants were once sung by
all the people, but now there were no composers *(poetae)* in Germany
capable of providing suitable chants in the vernacular for the people.[2]

By 1526, Luther accepted the need for further revision and
produced the text of his *Deutsche Messe*, most of which was in
German. In the introduction, he expresses the wish that his previous
Latin mass should still be used, but in the German mass simplicity
should prevail in the chants and in the ritual. The traditional Kyrie is
retained, but the Sanctus and Agnus are to be in German. There
should be a German hymn between the epistle and the gospel, which
is followed by the Creed (these three sung in German).

Taken with what he said about the freedom to retain symbols such
as candles or vestments, the somewhat mixed message given by
Luther in these liturgical innovations had in the long run the effect
of creating a Lutheran liturgy into which much of the former
liturgical music fitted. Catholic composers wrote music for the
Lutheran liturgy because the idiom was similar in many ways. The
masses of Josquin des Prés fitted into a Lutheran framework because
they had been composed for a liturgy in which the Canon was silent,
and the offertory, to which Luther objected, could be assigned a

motet and not become part of the integrated mass composition. The polyphonic mass, which 'was all sacrament and no sacrifice'[3] could then be regarded as a pure embodiment of the sacred by Lutherans, and its appeal did in fact continue, so that it is not a surprise that Bach should have composed a mass.

But in this way an important transition took place. Such masses, freed from their attachment to a liturgical theology, could assume the character of a spiritual concert and seem to have done so in the churches of Lutheran Germany. Those who listened no longer did so quite as a worshipping body, though something more than an audience. Thus, it would seem, the quasi-sacred institution of the modern concert was born.

Luther's reform opened the way too for German hymns. The books that appeared almost immediately demonstrate this clearly. The history of Protestant hymnals begins in fact with the *Achtliederbuch* of the Nuremberg printer Jobst Gutknecht in 1523–4, containing four hymns by Luther himself.

Huldrych Zwingli

Despite agreement on the defining theological questions of the Reformation, such as justification by faith and the sufficiency of Scripture, there were differences between the positions of the principal Reformers on important theological issues, most notably on the eucharist, and consequently differences in their conceptions of liturgical worship. The contrast is greatest between Luther's conservative liturgy and the reductionist approach of Huldrych Zwingli (1484–1531), whose understanding of the eucharist was that it was simply a commemorative meal, whereas Luther held a doctrine of 'real presence'. The contrast extends to their attitude towards music in the liturgy and this shows the influence of their respective theological positions as they were both musically quite literate: each of them had a good singing voice and played several instruments.[4] But Zwingli frequently made pejorative remarks about church music.[5] He did approve of simple, monotone chanting, but he made no effort to encourage congregational singing (of the psalms, for example) and famously caused the organs to be removed from the churches of Geneva,[6] while Luther wanted 'to see all the arts, especially music, used in the service of him who gave and made them'.[7]

Various reasons can be given for Zwingli's iconoclastic attitude – to all of liturgical ceremonial as well as to music. The most fundamental one is perhaps indicated by his preference for the scripture text, John 6:63: 'It is the spirit that gives life, the flesh is of no avail.' This text he saw as support for direct unmediated conferring of grace by the Holy Spirit and for his disparagement of all mediation by external rites. His was a dualistic approach that involved a distrust of material things where the relationship with God was concerned. Images in churches were idols, organs a distraction, singing made it more difficult to attend to the word of God itself.

His first reform of the liturgy might therefore be expected to be very radical, but in fact he feared a reaction from those who were 'weaker in the faith'[8] and the rite described in his *De Canone Missae Epicheiresis* (1523), while theologically a fundamental departure from the tradition, was not much changed in externals. Vestments were retained, the language (except for the lessons) was Latin, but four new prayers took the place of the official Canon of the mass. The Kyrie, Gloria, Sanctus, Agnus Dei were retained, sung by a choir, who still had the use of the organ for some time after the great clearing out of the churches of all images, altars, and ornaments was undertaken by a team of craftsmen under the supervision of the city architect in June 1524.[9]

As Luther was finding in the same period in Germany, Zwingli's reform of the mass satisfied neither conservatives nor radicals, and by the following Easter the Council of Zürich decided to abolish the traditional mass and replace it with a communion service in accordance with the theology of the eucharist that Zwingli had been promoting. Zwingli was ready with his new order of service, *Action oder Brauch des Nachtmahls,* and this came into use on Holy Thursday. Ceremonies were reduced to the barest minimum; it was no longer the mass but the 'Lord's Supper', a fellowship meal with the participants sitting around a table in the nave. In the new rite the principal elements were introductory prayers and sermon, the epistle and the gospel, an exhortation to devout communion, the Lord's

Prayer, a prayer of 'humble access' and the Narrative of Institution. As first published, the Gloria was included, to be said antiphonally, but this was omitted from 1529, so that none of the traditional sung elements remained. The organ was removed from the principal church, the Great Minster, in 1527, other smaller instruments having being removed from various churches in the previous three years.[10] (The organ was restored to the Minster only in 1874.)

Music was thus effectively removed from the Zürich liturgy and what evidence exists of religious music published in the first phase of the Reformation there seems to pertain to domestic rather than church use.

After Zwingli's death in 1531, the church there gradually came under the influence of the reform promoted by Calvin at Geneva and these and other cities of Switzerland developed what became known as the Reformed tradition, distinct from the Lutheran in theological and organisational terms and in musical tradition.

Calvinism

John Calvin (1509–1564) came to Geneva after the Reformation had already taken hold there, but he was the dominant figure in the movement for more than twenty years up to his death.

Initially an admirer of Luther's teaching (on the basic Reformation doctrine of justification, for example), he developed his own views in a series of editions of his *Institutes of the Christian Religion* (1536–1559). His teaching on the eucharist was strongly opposed to that of Luther, while yet quite different from that of Zwingli. His liturgical reform, however, was, like that of Zwingli, a radical departure from the medieval tradition.

As pastor of the French-speaking church in Strasbourg from 1538 to 1541, having been exiled by the Genevans, he experienced the singing of psalms by the congregation in metrical form. This led him in 1539 to publish *Aulcunes pseulmes et cantiques mys en chant*, a collection of French translations of psalms made by a French poet, Marot, and by himself, and set to tunes in use by the German-speaking church in the city. This was the first step towards what was to become the well-known Genevan Psalter. This complete French Psalter, *Pseulmes de David* (1562), contained 125 tunes, seventy of which were composed by Louis Bourgeois (d. 1600). It was published in Paris because Calvin objected to the harmonisations Bourgeois wanted to include in it.[11] Calvin wished the people to sing only an unadorned melody line.

Calvin has the reputation, not entirely unearned, of being grimly austere in his personal life and of having imposed such a regime on Geneva, once his authority there was firmly established (which only obtained in fact for the last ten years of his life). Some of his reforms at the social level were in fact unsuccessful and it is known that music and dancing went on in private to some extent as before.[12] He did regulate church life in detail and did find a place for music in it, in accordance with his well thought-out views expressed in the *Institutes*. For him, public prayer and singing, unless they sprang from deep feeling of the heart, had no value or profit with God. 'We do not here condemn speaking and singing but rather strongly commend them, provided they are associated with the heart's affection. . . . Moreover, since the glory of God ought, in a measure, to shine in the several parts of our bodies, it is especially fitting that the tongue has been assigned and destined for this task, both through singing and through speaking. For it was peculiarly created to tell and proclaim the praise of God.'[13] On the other hand, 'such songs as have been composed only for sweetness and delight of the ear are unbecoming to the majesty of the church and cannot but displease God in the highest degree.'[14] It could be said that there is here as much a distrust of beauty as there is a defence of sobriety, but the effect of Calvin's attitude and strict regulation of music in the Genevan liturgy was the creation of a unique 'sacred style' and the relegation to the secular sphere of all art music. This division appeared in the Lutheran world somewhat later than in Calvinism.

The form taken by Calvin's liturgy was given in his *La forme des prières et chants ecclésiastiques* . . .[15] (1542). The eucharist began with penitential prayer, followed by the singing of 'a psalm' *(psalmus aliquisx)*[16] unaccompanied (as in Zürich). Prayers and readings, a sermon, intercessions, an exhortation, followed before the bread and wine were distributed, while again a psalm was sung. A prayer of thanksgiving and a blessing concluded the service. The rites for baptism and for ordination make no mention of singing and are notable for a stated wish to avoid all superfluous ceremony, so that even the imposition of hands in ordination may be omitted because of the danger of superstition.

The dominant feature of Geneva's life of worship, as in Zürich, was the daily sermon in the early morning, lasting 'the best part of an hour' and with no congregational singing.[17] This austere liturgy was to become the model for the reform promoted in Scotland by John Knox (1513–1572) and the Church of Scotland still belongs to the Calvinist, now called Presbyterian, tradition.

Calvinism was also influential in England up to the middle of the seventeenth century, being called Puritanism there, and two views of the church competed for over a century, but the mainstream English Reformation resulted in the dominance of a theological and liturgical tradition proper to the Church of England.

Anglicanism
Thomas Cranmer (1489–1556) was influenced by Lutheran ideas and had visited Germany before being nominated Archbishop of Canterbury by Henry VIII. His full programme of reform came with the publication, and imposition on the parishes, of the first edition of the *Book of Common Prayer* in 1549. Cranmer's principles of reform and consequent liturgical revision were initially similar to those of Luther, except that he introduced an entirely vernacular liturgy from the outset. He was also more comprehensive in his treatment of the liturgy in that the book included the liturgy of the hours as well as the rites of the church, including the eucharist. The Kyrie, Gloria, Sanctus/Benedictus and Agnus Dei were to be sung, by a choir of 'clerks', in English. John Merbecke (d. 1585) then issued his *Booke of Common Prayer,* noted in 1550 with melodies to fit the English words.

A new version of the book revised in accordance with Reformed theology appeared in 1552. The choral sections of the eucharist, now changed in name from Mass to Holy Communion, were reduced. There remained the Creed and the Gloria, the latter transferred to the end of the service. The Kyrie became a single petition following each of the Ten Commandments. A modified Sanctus, without Benedictus, was included but it was rarely used polyphonically, if at all.[18] The trend towards simplification was halted by Elizabeth I in 1559 and the Prayerbook finally reached the form it was to retain until modern times only in 1662. The musical settings gradually introduced were not affected by these theological revisions, as the Church of England liturgy from the beginning maintained a recognisable continuity in form with the medieval liturgy on which it was based. There were tensions, however, between those who, like Queen Elizabeth, wished to retain more 'Catholic' forms in the liturgy, and the Puritans, who sought further purification of the rites along the lines of the Genevan reform.

The Puritan influence was more easily exerted away from the centres of royal power and in the less endowed places of worship, notably rural parishes. Thus two kinds of liturgy existed, differing according to the degree of ceremonial and the use of such resources as choirs and organs. The more elaborate liturgy was of course to be found in the cathedrals, establishing a tradition of excellence that has endured. A Royal Injunction was issued by Elizabeth in 1559 encouraging more use of music in the parishes. A hymn or song of praise 'in the best sort of melody and music that may conveniently be devised' should be sung before or after morning prayer and evensong, provided that the words were understandable.[19] Humble parish churches were unlikely to have boasted an organ or choir and psalm-singing was the principal musical exercise.[20] *The Whole Book of Psalms,* published by Day of London in 1562 contained single-line melodies for the English translation made by Sternhold and Hopkins.

English church music developed remarkably during Elizabeth's reign. Musical settings of the canticles used at morning prayer and evensong were introduced and called the 'service'. The introduction of the anthem, a motet-like work usually based on psalm verses, came about as a result of Elizabeth's Injunction and gave opportunity to such composers as Thomas Tallis (d. 1585). His 'one note-per-syllable principle, devoid of verbal repetition, became the classic model of the English service and anthem style that was to persist up through the Victorian period'.[21] He also provided settings for four voices for Archbishop Parker's *The Whole Psalter translated into English metre,* published in 1567. Ironically, the greatest composer of the Elizabethan period in Anglican cathedral music was the Roman Catholic, William Byrd (d. 1623). Among the famous names, such as Richard Farrant, Christopher Tye, Thomas Morley, of this golden age of English music, was Orlando Gibbons (d. 1623), who in the uncertain religious conditions of the time is thought to have changed his allegiance, more than once.

During the middle of the seventeenth century there was virtually no development of church music in England because of the Civil War and the Puritan Commonwealth. With the restoration of the monarchy in 1660 there was a return to cathedral music and a momentary flourishing of service- and anthem-writing. The best composers of the Restoration period, John Blow (d. 1708) and Henry Purcell (d. 1695), put their best church music writing into anthems.[22] Anthem-writing continued into the early eighteenth century, notably in the work of George Frederick Handel (d. 1759), who was much influenced by Purcell. The oratorios of Handel, while based on biblical texts or stories, were intended to be dramatic works performed in theatres, usually during Lent when the opera and theatrical season was suspended.

Music flourished in the parishes as well as well as in the cathedrals during the Restoration in England. There was an increase in the number of organs in churches and with them groups of amateur singers to lead the psalmody. They were sometimes accompanied by various musical instruments, especially 'fiddles', and this amateur music-making became a significant force in the social life of country parishes, as Thomas Hardy's novels demonstrate for the nineteenth century.[23]

Methodism

It would appear that the real state of the Church of England, at least in the eighteenth century, belied the idyllic picture presented by Hardy. Certainly, the pastoral care in the urban centres fell far short of what might be expected in an established church so well furnished with cathedrals and clergy. The church was also affected by the rationalism of the Enlightenment, which had the effect of impoverishing the spirit of liturgical worship. John Wesley (1703–1791) was a Church of England priest who underwent a conversion experience and devoted the remainder of his life to evangelisation, especially among the most deprived social classes. He conducted revivalist meetings in the open air, but his movement gradually acquired buildings and assumed the form of a separate community from the Church of England. This developed into the Methodist Church and spread to the United States. Methodist worship was characterised by hymn-singing expressive of the heartfelt convictions of new converts and was greatly enhanced by hymns written for this purpose by Wesley's brother, Charles (d. 1788). The Wesleys favoured hymns over metrical psalms and part-singing and insisted that they be accessible to all. These hymns were of enormous importance in creating a Methodist identity, 'for the theology of the Methodist movement was essentially encapsulated in hymnic form, with the hymns functioning as agents of evangelism and catechesis as well as vehicles for the praise of God in divine worship.'[24] In contrast, John Wesley considered Anglican worship in his day to be stale and spiritless and spoke in 1757 of 'the screaming of boys who bawl out what they neither feel nor understand, or the unseasonable and unmeaning impertinence of a voluntary on the organ.' When Methodists sang, they did so 'with the spirit and with the understanding also, not in the miserable, scandalous doggerel of Hopkins and Sternhold'.[25] It is worth noting that the singing of hymns by the congregation in the Anglican liturgy did not receive official sanction in the Church of England until 1792.

About 1760, the Wesley brothers produced a hymn-book, *Select Hymns with Tunes Annext,* a book that included 'Directions for Singing'. In 1780 they produced the *Collection of Hymns,* containing 525 hymns, which were not ordered according to the liturgical calendar but were under various headings related to religious experience. As a service book, Wesley published in 1784 *The Sunday Service of the Methodists in North America,* an adaptation or abridgement of the Anglican Prayerbook. This began to be used in England also along with the various books of hymns, though ministers had considerable freedom in relation to the forms of worship and this continued up to modern times.

Conclusion

The liturgical traditions described up to now changed little until the mid-twentieth century when modern sensibilities began to find archaic forms, especially of language, burdensome.

In parallel with a similar movement in the Catholic Church, liturgical renewal has had considerable influence on nearly all religious traditions stemming from the Reformation and this has resulted in a convergence of worship patterns. New forms of celebration have led to the need for new worship books with new hymns, and in many cases new hymnals have been provided. Overall, through increasing use of musical versions of texts that might otherwise be spoken, music is now better integrated into worship in churches that have their roots in the sixteenth-century Reformation.

Notes

1. John Bossy, *Christianity in the West, 1400–1700* (Oxford: Oxford University Press, 1985), p. vii.
2. B.J. Kidd, *Documents of the Continental Reformation* (Oxford: Clarendon Press, 1911), p. 131.
3. John Bossy, op. cit., p. 165
4. Roland Bainton, *Here I Stand: Martin Luther* (Oxford: Lion Books, 1978), p. 340; Jean Rilliet, *Zwingli: Third Man of the Reformation,* trans. by H. Knight (London: Lutterworth Press 1964), p. 25.
5. In the Second Dispute (about reform) at Zürich, 27 October 1523, he said: 'Since chant and vestments both distract us from true prayer, that is, the raising of the mind to God, they are to be removed, in the right way and at the right time'. B.J. Kidd, op. cit., p. 436 (translation mine).
6. Gäbler, *Ulrich Huldrych Zwingli: His Life and Work,* trans. by Ruth Gritsch (Edinburgh: T.&T. Clark, 1986), p. 107
7. Luther in his 'Preface to the Wittenberg Hymnal' in *Luther's Works,* ed. by Ulrich Leupold, (Philadelphia: Fortress Press, 1965), III, p. 316.
8. R.C.D. Jasper, and G.J. Cuming, *Prayers of the Eucharist: Early and Reformed* (Collegeville: Liturgical Press, 1987), p. 181.
9. Bernard Reardon, *Religious Thought in the Reformation* (London: Longman, 1981), p. 95.
10. Timothy George, *Theology of the Reformers* (Nashville: Broadman & Holman, 1988), p. 131.
11. Frank Senn, *Christian Liturgy: Catholic and Evangelical* (Minneapolis: Fortress Press, 1997), p. 368.

12. Robert M. Kingdon, *Adultery and Divorce in Calvin's Geneva* (Cambridge, Mass.: Harvard University Press, 1995), pp. 100–1.

13. *Institutes of the Christian Religion,* trans. by F.L. Battles, III.xx.31 (Philadelphia: Westminster Press, 1960), II, p. 894.

14. Ibid., III.xx.32, p. 896.

15. The full title was: *Forme des priéres et chants ecclésiastiques., avec la manière d'administrer les sacrements et consacrer le mariage selon la coutume de l'Église ancienne.*

16. B.J. Kidd, op. cit., p. 616.

17. T.H.L. Parker, *John Calvin* (Berkhamsted: Lion Publishing, 1975), p. 109.

18. *Oxford Dictionary of the Reformation,* ed. by Hans Hillerbrand, (New York: 1996), III, p. 107.

19. H. Benham, *Latin Church Music in England 1460–1575* (London: Da Capo Press, 1977), p. 165.

20. Andrew Wilson-Dickson, *The Story of Christian Music* (Oxford: Lion Books, 1992), p. 71

21. Frank Senn, op. cit., p. 519.

22. Frank Senn, op. cit., p. 520.

23. For example, *Under the Greenwood Tree.*

24. *The Sunday Service of the Methodists,* ed. by Karen Tucker, (Nashville: Kingswood Books) p. 29.

25. *The Letters of John Wesley,* ed. by John Telford, (London: Epworth Press, 1931), III, p. 228.

THE SOUND OF GOD

Nóirín Ní Riain

THE AIM OF THIS EXPLORATION is to situate the phenomenological perception of sound within the broad context and realm of mystical revelation. There are two crucial questions: Can an anthropomorphic knowledge of God reveal and manifest itself through 'theosony'[1] as distinct and separate from human effort or thought? Within the overall cyclic life-pattern where the believer's quest for God is nurtured, can sound can be a central, crucial medium? My answer is yes. One might say in an initial, terse, summarising statement that Divine revelation is present and proposed to the finite world in such a way as to be heard and listened to through the medium of sound.

In the empirical context of the dialogue between Divine pursuit and human response, this article will focus critically on the power of sound to evoke that sense of transcendence necessary to bring this state, the religious experience,[2] to fruition. A keen attentiveness to sound, in any of its myriad apparitions and manifestations on both an individual and social level, enables one to become more what God wants us to be. 'Man does not search out God, but rather the reverse is true.'[3] Sound is a real link to one's divine and human essence and to the yearning to be oneself. Only by such becoming can we be more unified and thus participate in the two-way dialogue in freedom, which God generously offers.[4]

The mode of procedure in this theoretical[5] overview will be as follows: Firstly, a brief history of Christian Mysticism and its dual-stranded Jewish/Hellenist matrix to set the socio-historical backdrop for the Christian mystic; then, the fundamental religious facets of experience, using imagination through symbol and allegory – all either consciously or subliminally present to 'the person with the genius for God'[6] finally, in the contemporary universal call to the mystical encounter – in the actualisation of the encounter where the self and God are somehow one[7] – an aural theology, a theosonic happening that presents a new, yet unexplored and undervalued, path of Divine encounter.

The brief historical overview of Christian mysticism will do little more than outline three major panoramic movements or directions that the practice of Christian spirituality has revealed since its inception.

Firstly, there was the monastic-centred period from the third and fourth centuries to the twelfth century. The monastic communities of this period were the first to experience and evaluate the mystical theology of, for instance, Origen and Augustine. The exegetical concepts of reading, meditating on, teaching and preaching the sacred biblical texts inherent in early Christianity with its Judaic/Hellenist roots – along with the celebration of the Eucharist and the sacraments – found an ideal setting in monasticism.

Then came the organic shift in thirteenth-century Europe to a 'new mysticism . . . the richest era [the period between 1200 and 1350] for the production of mystical literature in the whole of Christianity'.[8] Mystical perfection is now accessible to all who seek it and the mystic now, through the later Middle Ages and the Reformation, teaches this perfection, not through the lofty Latin of the clergy but in their mother tongue, the vernacular.

The third period is characterised by William Johnston as 'developed and enriched by the Spanish Carmelites of the sixteenth century,' but remaining 'basically unchanged from the fourteenth century until the Second Vatican Council.'[9]

The genesis of Christian mysticism, and indeed of the God-man religion itself, emerges from the matrix of a two-stranded society and culture: one strand represents the Jewish influence of Second Temple ritual[10] with its late Temple sacred books such as the apocalypses and the Hebrew bible, well developed by the second century BCE. The second strand is Hellenistic philosophical mysticism. The *idée fixe* of earliest Greek philosophy was the soul's restless quest for the Absolute Good. Such a state, according to Plato,[11] involving the indwelling in the Divine One, is achieved through contemplation *(theoria),* which is bathed and purified in knowledge and love. Here is the throbbing heart of the contemplative ideal and part of the genesis of Christian mysticism. Greatly influenced by this Greek ideal, Philo (d. *c.* 50 CE), an Alexandrian Jew, integrated biblical monotheism into a school of mystical thought that emphasised the scriptural *logos*[12] as the Divine word mediating between the unknowable God and his subject.

Christian mysticism initially borrowed heavily exegetically, heuristically, ideologically and conceptually through a process of enculturation to which it freely and easily adapted. 'The profoundest contemplative experience of the ancient world entered into Christianity, where it was purified and completed.'[13] Jesus Christ was the *logos* – the true incarnate *theophania theou.* The heavenly state could be attained through the God-man present who since his ascension to his heavenly realm is still present in word and ritual to his believers.

Community worships God – *per-sona Christi* – empowered by the Holy Spirit through active participation in gestural speech and symbolic action.

A religious experience[14] is a particular instance of personally encountering the sacred, the transcendent. This religious dimension in human experience comes as a gift of insight into the presence of God. The fascination that Divine Reality holds, marks a permanent milestone in the story of all human existence. The storyteller in this sense is the mystic who struggles to articulate this obsession and its actualisation. Religious imagination – both for the mystic and the aspiring one – relies almost exclusively on finite reality and expression, which can provide only a very inadequate mirror-image of the Infinite.

A new interpretation, a new listening to mundane sound could reveal an aural formulation of the insatiable thirst inherited, irrespective of place and time in history. Although sound is not an exclusive channel of God's grace, it can be a central symbol and privileged means of encounter. Attaining the graced moment of mystical participation, faith-sound can lead to self-transcendence. Most authentic human experience of faith is related to and influenced by previous experience. So too, one's experience of heard and self-created sound is related to previous experience. Theosonance

– the condition or quality of being spiritually sonant – is the religious dimension of human hearing. It is a way of understanding self and reality through sound in relation to the divine. Through the medium of human sound, one remains present to religious experience. Theosony, as such, is the somehow definable sacred and transcendent sound that is accessible to human beings in their historical, concrete existence. Such sacred sound should be reflected upon within the context of the characteristics of sound in human experience in general.

Religious experience is not just dependent upon or achieved through traditional religious mediation alone. Mundane, everyday, familiar sounds around us can convey ultimate reality[15] – and perhaps more so – than sounds birthed out of religious fervour. All sound contains the possibility of new self-understanding.

Theosony transcends sensual and intellectual experience even though encounters with the divine will involve the senses and the intellect. Theosony as religious experience is ultimately pre-conceptual and beyond words and can only be defined in terms of concepts, images, analogies and symbols. The effect, not the process, is the ultimate focus. The context, not the content, becomes the agent whereby the *'per-sona humana'* participates in the life of the *'per-sona Dei'*. We are allowed to perceive beyond the world to that prior and salvific all-encompassing reality. Indeed the discernment of that *mysterium tremendum et fascinans* – in the phrase coined by Rudolf Otto in 1923[16] – is enhanced through the transitional object of sound as a potential space for such encounter. Sound is temporal, coming into existence at the moment of its passing away, shimmering between being and non-being, more an event than an object, a verb rather than a noun.

Symbolism is a primary category in Christian life, working as metaphors do in awakening an encounter with an ultimate other at the limits of human existence. Symbolic and analogical discourse allow, enhance and protect a finite perception and understanding of the *apeiron* or the Infinite. Unconditional acceptance of a Divine or numinous quality is quiescent until aroused by some symbol that triggers it into activity. Sound can be such a symbol awakening this latent tendency. When true theosony manifests itself, it becomes an incontrovertible symbolic moment of God's disclosure to those who hear.

Theosony can be both symbolic medium and expression – medium in that it arouses the profound yearning towards God, and expression as the means of living it out when aroused. Can theosony be integral to the manifestation and specification of this original sacrament of Christ – the ultimate symbol? Sound is a sign of God's self-communication and self-revelation through Christ's paschal mystery in certain symbolic acts and words. Theosony looks through and away from the symbol to the Divine, which it re-sonates. Theosonantally, God reveals and grants salvation through Christ's paschal mystery in sonantal symbols.

Theosonic symbolism is rooted in and emanates from a theological interpretation of sound symbolism[17] whereby the representation of theological sense or meaning of a word is dependent on the sound or enunciation of the word. Broadening the wider web of sound symbolism, which generally confines itself to phonetics or the science of words, theological symbolism depends on the awareness of the hearer enhanced through the agency of the Holy Spirit, which allows it to transcend linguistic, social, cultural or ethnic boundaries. Allegory, the figurative presentation of spiritual meaning in concrete forms, transports the mystic through recurring images. Images of flame, cloud, darkness, night, light – the allegorical vocabulary unfolds as we are shocked into 'the consciousness of God's presence.'[18]

The way of the mystic who seeks 'to translate the truth of that world into the beauty of this'[19] involves a three-fold process. First there is a time of preparation where one, through sounds, words and concepts, dons 'the clothing which the spiritual borrows from the material plane'.[20] This may herald what the great Spanish sixteenth-century mystic Teresa of Avila[21] called a prayer of quiet – a personal, painful encounter with the Divine. Interpretation of, or reaction to, this consciousness of 'the living flame of love'[22] may or may not present a pastoral element that will be the decision or choice to communicate this being in love with God to other human beings. Whether it does or does not in no way diminishes the universal call to mysticism.

'The devout Christian of the future will either be a mystic, one who has "experienced" something, or will cease to be anything at all.'[23] This radical prognosis of Karl Rahner[24] voices the 'cri de coeur' of many contemporary theologians for a metanoia of vision towards a new dimension of 'doing' theology.[25]

The phenomenon of mystical consciousness of the presence of God, its historicity, is our guarantee of the end towards which the Immanent Love – 'the hidden steersman'[26] – is moving us. Theosony is the keen perception of an obedient listening[27] to the indwelling of the Absolute – when the heart is lifted up to God 'with a meek stirring of love'.[28] It is an obedience of humility to the will and word of God. It is the moment the psalmist sings of, when 'the voice of the Lord is heard over the waters when the glorious God, thunders' (Ps 28). The same 'still small voice' (1 Kings 19:12)[29] of God, that moved Elijah to cover his face and take flight, transforms the ordinary world into one single, ineffable act of perception and listening, where sound, sight, touch, taste and smell merge into aspects of one thing – a Divine sensual fusion.

Mysticism is a process, an organic process, that proceeds from a unique personal encounter with God and subsequently moulds and sculpts one's *Tao* or way[30] in love and wisdom. Organic, in that the ultimate reality of this divine/human encounter is dynamic, 'that it moves towards us as we move towards it, that it searches us out before we go in search of it'.[31] True theosony discloses itself to the human person in a way that is not manipulable. It creates an embryo of listening rather than questioning or speaking. It is a liberating power of sound, the imaginative space of hearing proclaimed and heralded by Moses 'the greatest of mystics'[32]:

> Surely, this commandment that I am commanding you today is not too hard for you, nor is it too far away. It is not in heaven, that you should say, 'Who will go up to heaven for us, and get it for us so that we may hear it and observe it?' Neither is it beyond the sea, that you should say, 'Who will cross to the other side of the sea for us, and get it for us so that we may hear it and observe it?' No, the word is very near to you; it is in your mouth and in your heart for you to observe it. (Deut 30:11–14)

Notes

1. A portmanteau word derived from the Greek for God and the Latin for sound. This essay is a first sketch of a more developed thesis that I am exploring presently.

2. The characteristics of religious experience were delineated by William James at the Gifford lectures that he delivered at Edinburgh in 1901–1902, later published in *The Varieties of Religious Experience* (Glasgow: Collins, 1977). Evelyn Underhill in *Mysticism* (London: Methuen, 1911) firmly opposes James. She emphasises a more pragmatic interpretation of religious experience centred on the spiritual nature of the activity emanating from love, and the psychological experience of the entire self, which is not self-seeking in this instance.

3. John Macquarrie, *On Being a Theologian* (London: SCM Press, 1994), p. 53.

4. See the writings of the Swiss theologian Hans Urs Von Balthasar (1905–1988), particularly *Herrlichkeit, III/I, Im Raum der Metaphysik* (Einsiedeln: Johannes, 1965), pp. 221, 260. The sound of music was an integral part of this theologian's being – his youth was 'pervaded by music' he himself wrote (*Unser Auftrag, Bericht und Entwurf,* Einsiedeln:Johannes, 1983, p. 31) and he apparently knew all the music of Mozart by heart. (see Introduction Thomas G. Dalzell, *The Dramatic Encounter of Divine and Human Freedom in the Theology of Hans Urs von Balthasar,* Germany: Peter Lang, p. 13.)

5. As well as referring to the conceptual and abstract connotation of this word, the original derivation of the word 'theory' is from the Greek neoplatonic word 'theoria', which means a 'seeing', 'a gazing' or a 'contemplation'. The Greek word is almost synonymous with God himself because Theos, the positive name of God, is thought to derive from 'theastai' (to behold). See Bernard McGinn, *The Foundations of Christian Mysticism* (NY: Crossroad, 1999), p. 179. Furthermore, I use it carefully to synthesise both seeing and hearing, listening or sounding as means towards revelation.

6. Evelyn Underhill, *Mysticism* (London: Methuen, 1911), p. 104. This is her definition of a true mystic.

7. Many fundamental theologians over the past few decades have addressed this question of the universality of the mystical experience from both sides of the debate. Cuthbert Butler OSB in his classic book *Western Mysticism* (NY: Dutton, 1923) was one of the first to insist that all Christians are in some way called to mystical experience. On this particular point of the union of self and God knowledge in particular, see Karl Rahner, *Theological Investigations* (London: Darton, 1961), XIII, pp. 122–136.

8.   Bernard McGinn, *The Flowering of Mysticism* (New York: Crossroad Publications), p. x. 'New Mysticism' is McGinn's own terminology for this 'layer' (his preferred word to 'period') of Western Christian mysticism.

9.   William Johnston, *Mystical Theology* (Maryknoll, NY: Orbis Books, 1995), p. 53.

10. Although this period spans from 515BCE to 70CE, it was the later years that were most influential.

11. To label Plato a mystic is controversial but McGinn has 'no hesitation in doing so'. See *The Foundations of Mysticism*, p. 25.

12. This word was first used in pagan Greek thought by Heraclitus of Ephesus, sixth century BCE and in its Christian usage from the classic Prologue to the Gospel of John (1:1–18), where it assumes an incarnate logos – a theosonic *theophania theou.*

13. Friedrich Heiler 'Contemplation in Christian Mysticism', *Spiritual Disciplines: Papers from the Eranos Yearbooks* (New York: Pantheon, 1960), p. 192. Evelyn Underhill concurs.

14. This term was first used in a technical context by William James in *Varieties of Religious Experience.*

15. I use this term in the context of the definition of ultimate reality by the Protestant exile theologian, Paul Tillich (1886–1965). For him, ultimate reality 'becomes manifest through ecstatic experiences of a concrete-revelatory character and is expressed in symbols and myths'. See 'Art and Ultimate Reality' (lecture 1959, first published 1960), in Paul Tillich, *Main Works,* ed. by Michael Palmer (New York: De Gruyter, Evangelisches Verlagswerk, 1990), II, p. 318.

16. Rudolf Otto, *The Idea of the Holy* (London: Penguin, 1959), p. 32.

17. Sound symbolism refers to those words that by their very sounding resemble the sense or meaning of the word, e.g., buzz, bang. Phonetically based, the very words of God/Theos/Deus also carry sonantally the sense of transcendence, awe and immanence pertinent to theological speculation.

18. Bernard McGinn, *The Flowering of Mysticism,* p.xi. McGinn uses this definition as the deeper and most immediate understanding of Christian mysticism. Teresa of Avila, in writing of what she felt was mystical theology '. . . a consciousness of the presence of God of such a kind that I could not possibly doubt that he was within me or that I was wholly engulfed in him.' *The Life of Teresa of Jesus: The Autobiography of St. Teresa of Avila,* trans. and ed. by E. Allison Peers (New York: Doubleday), p.119.

19. Evelyn Underhill, *Mysticism,* p. 80.

20. Ibid., p.80

21. Teresa of Avila is recognised (much through the pioneering attention to this by Auguste Poulain, d. 1919) as the first mystic to articulate the early states of consiousness before the mystical experience. See *The Interior Castle* trans. by E. Allison Peers (NY: Doubleday, 1961); *The Way of Perfection*, trans. by E. Allison Peers (NY: Doubleday, 1964).

22. Title of a mystical treatise of St John of the Cross – see *The Selected Works of St John of the Cross,* trans. by Kavanaugh/Rodriguez (Washington DC: Inst. of Carmelite Studies, 1973).

23. Karl Rahner, *Theological Investigations,* VII, p. 15. Also called 'Doctor mysticus' of the twentieth century (Harvey D. Egan SJ in Rahner's *I Remember an Autobiographical Interview with Meinhold Kraus* (NY: Crossroad, 1985), p. 3), he highlighted the necessity to do theology that is rooted in the mystical experience of all faithful Christians.

24. Rahner's (d. 1984) theology has been described as 'the most significant Catholic writing on mysticism of the recent decades'. See McGinn, *Foundations*, p. 285.

25. I refer here to a call from Dr Peter Heunnerman, Tubingen University, Germany, at a theological conference in Waterford in November 2000. Towards the conclusion of his address he highlighted the urgent necessity of a new approach to theology that would merge the two areas of dogmatic and mystical theology.

26. Underhill, *Mysticism*, p. 450.

27. The words obedience and listen are apparently derived from the Latin *ob audire,* which means to listen intently. So a listening implies an obedience to the sound and its message. In the Book of the Apocalypse alone – *Apocalypse* being the Greek word for Revelation – three times the command to listen and hear the sound of the spirit is clearly enunciated. 'Let anyone who has an ear listen to what the Spirit is saying . . .' (Rev 2:7; 3:6,13.) See also Matthew, 11:15. The most influential school of Christian Western Mysticism, formulated in St Benedict's *Rule*, begins with the exhortation to 'listen carefully. . . . and attend with the ear of your heart'. Prologue:1 *The Rule of St Benedict in English* (Collegeville, Minn: Liturgical Press, 1981), p. 15.

28. *Cloud of Unknowing*, ed. by Evelyn Underhill (Rockland, MA: Element, 1997), ch. 3, l. 1, p. 53.

29. This description of one of the earliest aural theophanies also appears as 'the sound of the gentle breeze', 'sound of sheer silence' (NRSV).

30. As well as its relevance to oriental thought, it is also deeply biblical, occurring 880 times in Septuagint, i.e., Old Testament Greek. It also appears in Synoptics, John and Paul. As in the orient, 'way' is figurative.

31. William Johnston, *Silent Music* (Suffolk: Collins, 1974), p. 49.

32. William Johnston, *Arise My Love…* (NY: Orbis, 2000), p. 116. Elijah, mentioned above, also shares this definition.

AESTHETICS, SCIENCE AND HEALING

Towards a Definition of 'Good' Liturgical Music

Gerard Gillen

THE RELATIONSHIP BETWEEN the Church's formal patterns of worship, the liturgy, and the arts in general, but music in particular, continues to be one of the most complex and problematic issues for the Church as it seeks to advance the trajectory of liturgical reform and renewal established by the Second Vatican Council. It is an age-old dilemma: we think of St Jerome's outbursts against the vanity of artists,[1] St Augustine's scruples in taking pleasure from the music of the psalms,[2] the archbishop of Salzburg's strong reining in of Mozart's natural compositional effervescence in his liturgical strictures on the composer,[3] and so on right down to the pastor who forbids his choir from singing the motet they most want to sing on the grounds that it is too long or inappropriate or both.

Liturgy and music have been symbiotically related to each other from Temple times: the numerous references to sung worship in the psalms serves as a basis for understanding this inextricable link between music and ritual usage:

> Sing Yahweh a new song
> let the congregation of the faithful sing his praise (Ps 149:1). . .
> Let them dance in praise of his name
> Playing to him on strings and drums (Ps 149:3)

And the *Canticle of Judith* commences:

> Praise my God with the Tambourine
> Sing to the Lord with the cymbal

Let psalm and canticle mingle for him
Extol his name, invoke it (Judith: 16)[4]

As archbishop Rembert Weakland, the eminent American
Benedictine liturgist has put it: 'Music is no appendage, no
decorative extra, or optional interlude.'[5] It is an essential element of
liturgical praise as it unveils a dimension of meaning and feeling, a
communication of ideas and intuitions that words alone cannot
yield. In other words, art helps us to express the inexpressible. All the
arts share this capacity, and as the artist Patrick Pye has put it, 'art
does not tell us what to believe, it tells us what it *feels* like to believe.'[6]

In 1972 the US Catholic Bishops' Committee on the Liturgy
issued a document entitled *Music in Catholic Worship,* which
established that three judgments should determine the
appropriateness of music for liturgical usage: the musical judgment,
the pastoral judgment, and the liturgical judgment.[7] Over the past
thirty years various attempts have been made to refine the criteria for
these judgments and to integrate their diverse concerns. Considerable
progress has been made in advancing the criteria for the pastoral and
liturgical judgments, but, not surprisingly, establishing criteria for
the musical judgment has proven more difficult. Frankly, there is
little current consensus in the Church on what constitutes 'good'
music, and there has in fact been little serious discussion on the issue
over the years given that it takes us into the deep waters of
theological, philosophical and aesthetic evaluation.

It was in 1903 that Pope Pius X in his celebrated *motu proprio* 'Tra
le Sollecitudini' set out three defining qualities of truly sacred music:
santita (holiness), *bonta del forma* (beauty or goodness of form) and
universalita, which was said to arise spontaneously from the other
two.[8] These categories of Pius X – holiness, beauty (goodness) of
form, and universality – set the parameters for Catholic discussions
of liturgical music for the entire twentieth century. In the same
document the pope also proposed a fourth characteristic of liturgical
music: that it should be a *parte integrante della solenne liturgia,* and,
therefore, must be *umile ancilla* to the liturgy. In other words Pius X
had set out the requirements that became basic to Vatican II's

liturgical reforms, that music be an integral part of the liturgical rites and, therefore, that it be *ritual* in character.

In discussing the aesthetics of liturgical music I feel it is useful to consider three of Pius X's four defining qualities, the fourth (universality) having been quietly dropped since Vatican II, if not before. For example, the 1967 Vatican Instruction *Musicam Sacram,* when quoting Pius X omits the term without explanation.[9]

Holiness

The question to be addressed here is whether the distinction between the sacred and profane in music is a valid one. Many today are concerned about the poor quality of much Catholic liturgical music. Is sacrality or holiness the element we are looking for to separate the good music from the bad? To distinguish qualitatively between sacred and secular music is hardly sustainable, although an apparent distinction of styles is commonly perceived to exist. It is historically true, of course, that the Church fathers were strongly opposed to pagan musical practices. There was hardly a Church father from the fourth century who did not inveigh in strong terms against pagan musical practices.[10] But we have no evidence of a *stylistic* difference between liturgical music and secular music in the patristic era or any later era for that matter. What we do have is a difference of repertoires. For example, in the fifteenth century the same vocal style was shared between sacred and secular composition (*cantus firmus* technique was common to both). Similarly, a century later one is unable to find any clear stylistic distinction between the mass compositions and secular madrigals of that so-called paragon of religious virtue in music, Palestrina. And in the centuries after Trent we find that each new development in musical composition found its way into worship music, with little stylistic difference between court, theatre or church. There are many blatant examples: Monteverdi borrowing the music from his prologue to *Orfeo* for the 'Deus in adjutorium' of his *Vespers.* And volumes literally have been written on the crossover elements between the sacred and secular music of Bach and Mozart.[11]

It is interesting that the first documented use of the term 'musica sacra' comes only in the seventeenth century, and from a Lutheran source (Michael Praetorius in 1614), where the distinction between sacred and secular music is not one of any *quality* or characteristic of the music, but one of *practice*, indicating the usage of specific compositions.[12] It would appear that it was in the first half of the nineteenth century with the advent of Romanticism that 'musica sacra' first came to mean 'holy sound'. This new term of 'music sacra' was made possible by the increasing use of the term *heilig* by German poets to encompass the 'sublime, mythological, religious'. Gradually, from the latter half of the nineteenth century onwards, this notion of 'holy' began to inform the term 'musica sacra', which became used to denote exemplary music such as Palestrina, which was to be revived in the face of the perceived secularisation of Church music. This revisionist notion of 'musica sacra antiqua' was greatly influenced by opponents of the Enlightenment, Liberalism, Socialism and Anti-clericalism. The first papal use of the term 'musica sacra' comes from Pius IX's apostolic brief of 1870 approving the statutes of the German Cecilian society.[13] The Cecilians, of course, were prominent in articulating the sacred/secular dichotomy as they understood it. The compositional result of their philosophic position was that a view became entrenched in the Church that promoted second and third-rate imitations of Palestrina for liturgical use on the grounds of sacrality, with Haydn, Mozart, and Bruckner rejected on ideological grounds.[14] And so the idea of 'musica sacra' is hardly a hallowed tradition of the Church, but one that has only relatively latterly become a polemical formula for a pseudo-traditional concept of Church music.

But the magisterium's 'musica sacra' position from 1903 to 1963 has hardly been a consistent one. For example, Pius X in his zeal to eliminate the profane, forbade the use of strings in liturgical contexts. But Pius XII (who played the violin) officially sanctioned their use in 1955.[15] Did such music, previously profane, now become sacred with the later papal approbation? In fact Pius X had a very restricted view on what constituted 'sacred music'. By 'musica sacra' he meant only Gregorian chant, classical polyphony, and modern pastiche polyphony; genres such as instrumental music or vernacular songs during processions were excluded. But the 1958 Roman instruction and the 1967 later instruction included the following under sacred music: Gregorian chant, sacred polyphony, modern sacred music, sacred organ music, popular religious singing (in the vernacular), and religious music. By now vernacular hymnody was accepted for liturgical use and was thus to be regarded as sacred. So there was obviously a considerable shift in papal thinking between the beginning and the latter half of the twentieth century; so much so that in continuing to use the term 'sacred music' (as the 1967 Vatican II instruction does) the impression is given that the papal documents do so by way of adherence to traditional language rather than out of conviction that some music is sacred and other profane, as Pius X had believed.[16]

So while the distinction between the 'sacred' and the 'secular' in music is not as simple and clearly-defined as the Pius X *Motu proprio* would have us believe, the alternative of an *à la carte* approach to the acceptance of music in the liturgy is clearly unsatisfactory. In many quarters, the years since Vatican II have seen a reaction to the 'sacred music' idea whereby virtually anything was countenanced in liturgical music in the name of pastoral need or cultural exigency. The problem now is to identify the inappropriate features of current liturgical music and establish reasons for their inadequacy.

In 1995 a group of English-speaking liturgists and musicians issued a comprehensive statement on music in the liturgy, which was published in the United States as the *Snowbird Statement*.[17] In article 7 of *Snowbird* this question is addressed as follows:

> While we believe that the process of dialogue between liturgy and its cultural context must be promoted and advanced, we challenge the indiscriminate incorporation of an entertainment or therapeutic ethos into liturgical music. . . . Particular dangers inherent in the adoption of currently popular musical styles and idioms are sentimentality, consumerism, individualism, introversion, and passivity.

And so the question we should ask ourselves is whether some styles of modern liturgical music conspicuously tend towards 'sentimentality, consumerism, individualism, introversion, and passivity'. The answer may very well be 'yes'. The category of contemporary liturgical music commonly referred to by the misnomer of 'folk' music, more accurately to be described as 'sacro-pop', springs to mind. As Anthony Ruff has argued: 'The logic of the *Snowbird Statement* would appear to lead to the difficult conclusion that it is not simply a question of choosing the best within each style, as is often asserted, but rather that some styles of music are problematic. In other words, even if there is no intrinsically 'sacred' music, there are grounds for critiquing harmful cultural influences which have found entrance into liturgical music in recent decades.'[18]

Beauty

The discussion of musical quality under this descriptive designation will be confined primarily to Western music, since its style and language is that normally employed by composers whose music is used in Western liturgical practice. This permits the possibility of qualitative comparisons between say, Mozart and John Foley and Haydn and Carey Landrey.

Article 6 of the *Snowbird Statement* states that: 'To the extent that many of the styles employed in English-language Catholic worship today are dialects of the same larger musical language (in terms of harmonic vocabulary or rhythmic organisation), a discussion of musical quality across stylistic boundaries is valid and necessary.' This comparison across styles refers only to music of different eras that share a common harmonic vocabulary and periodic structure, such as the *lingua franca* of Western or European music. So to the extent that Mozart or Edward Foley use a common eighteenth-century European harmonic musical vocabulary, there are grounds for comparison. But to the extent that their self-chosen musical vocabulary is different, one must be cautious in such trans-stylistic judgments. How therefore do we proceed in making a trans-stylistic comparison?

Once again Ruff gets to the core of the matter when he argues: 'It hardly needs to be emphasised in our day that aesthetic judgments are made from a particular social location, a limited viewpoint. Few would deny that we perceive only within the limitations of a culture, in a given time and place. But what implications must be drawn from this? Are aesthetic judgments nothing but expressions of social convention? Are we so influenced by our social location that we have absolutely no access to the objectively beautiful?'[19] Ruff goes on to argue that although it may be difficult to prove, it is surely possible that we humans have been given at least some access to objective beauty, at least some ability to judge beauty's presence. It is surely important to resist the total relativism that would reduce all aesthetic claims to personal preference, even if, or exactly because, such relativism fits very well with many features of popular culture today.

There are, therefore, two elements, as Ruff puts it. On the one side, that fact of 'cultural colouring' of all human judgment, on the other side, the unproven (and perhaps, unprovable) conviction that there is objective beauty to which we have at least some limited access. Any aesthetic reflection on Church music must give due weight to both sides if there is to be fruitful discussion of aesthetics in Catholic liturgical music. The most difficult element to discuss and prove is the conviction of limited access to objective beauty; even if unprovable it is surely an appropriate conviction for Christians to share and to employ as a basis for discussion.

By analogy, it could be said that what is written here about beauty is not unlike what Christians believe about God, in that our access to the Divine as creatures is limited; all God-language is analogical; for all our imagery, according to the Fourth Lateran Council, the dissimilarity to the reality is greater than the similarity. Aquinas's five proofs for the existence of God are more after-the-fact explication of an already held conviction than they are proofs held to be able to convince the non-believer. And yet we believe in God, and so we have theology as a discipline that probes, penetrates and postulates the implications of that belief. Our position with regard to aesthetics is much the same as that with regard to theology in that we start with an unprovable conviction of limited access to something believed to exist objectively.

If there are objective elements to aesthetic judgments, how do we define standards of judgment within the canon of Western music? What standards do we apply in trying to recognise musical quality? How is aesthetic sensitivity developed and formed? The process would appear to involve our encounter with the classics of a given tradition and the repertoire that others have judged to be of high quality. Exposure to playing, singing, studying and concentrated listening of canonic repertoire enables us to discover why *others* have found such music compelling. This is where trust and dialogue with those professionally trained in the subject becomes relevant. As article 6 of *Snowbird* puts it:

> There are those who, through talent and training, are able to identify music that is technically, aesthetically and expressively good. In seeking to judge musical quality, we could do well to consult the cumulative wisdom of both our contemporaries and our predecessors.

By such a process we develop a faculty or talent for discerning the musical substance of a piece, and by such a process we also develop the instinctive ability to recognise that a particular piece does *not* have substance, or that it is *not* profound or interesting. Through such a formative aesthetic process, built on the wisdom of others, we learn why *this* melodic repetition is interesting, but *that* one insipid, why *this* harmonic complexity is profound, but *that* one pretentious. The task, mostly communal, of discerning the objective elements in musical judgment is indeed a difficult one. It would be easier if there were clear-cut standards to apply, but unfortunately there are not. And as article 6 of *Snowbird* continues:

> The difficulty of definitely stating the objective elements of musical quality is not an excuse for avoiding the issue or proof of the relativity of musical judgments, but rather an indication of human incompleteness and an impetus to further conversation.

It is generally agreed that much of the music used in English-speaking Catholic worship is of poor quality. But to demonstrate satisfactorily its deficiencies is not such an easy task. The bases for aesthetic judgments are notoriously problematic. In making an assumption of high quality in regard to the classics of Western music, and in asserting (as *Snowbird* does) that some *through talent and training, are able to identify music that is technically, aesthetically and expressively good,* one leaves oneself open to the charge of élitist snobbery. As Ruff asserts: 'Liturgical music must of its very nature be popular, literally *people's* music.'[20] All music, whether a congregational hymn, a piece of Gregorian chant, a polyphonic Gloria, or an instrumental solo belongs to the assembly, but that is not to suggest that the requirement of high quality is in any way in conflict with that of simplicity.

Perhaps the aesthetics of seventeenth- and eighteenth-century Lutheran Germany are relevant. The hymnody developed by their musicians and liturgists was folk music in the real sense of the term, and became a basis for an entire culture of liturgical hymn-based choral and organ repertory.[21] Folk music and high-art music co-existed, not merely side by side, but in symbiotic relationship with each other, all of it belonging to the worshipping assembly. Thus the introduction into the liturgy of high-art music (be it instrumental or vocal) must not necessarily be branded as élitist. This is an attitude that, by its very nature, precludes the possibility of such music becoming part of the ownership of the assembly through repeated usage. In this way, music that is not necessarily sung by the assembly, but listened to attentively and meditated upon by an assembly that identifies with the music in question, becomes people's music at a very profound level.

Ritual music
It is often suggested that this last category belongs to a post Vatican II view of liturgical music. But this is not true, as Pius X held something very close to a 'ritual music' position with his teaching that music must be 'an integrated part of the solemn liturgy' and 'a holy handmaid of the liturgy'.[22] The notion is probably even older than 1903, and can be found at least implicitly in Solesmes's idealisation of chant in the nineteenth century as ideally suited to the Roman liturgy. Whatever the history of implicit or explicit convictions, the concept of 'ritual music' is absolutely necessary in any thinking about Catholic liturgical music today. Today's dilemma is to show that music of the past is relevant for today's rite, which, after all, is a different rite to that for which the music was originally conceived. In order to answer this, we have to ask the question: Does

this piece of music fit our liturgy, our understanding of rite, of beauty, of pastoral sensitivity, of communal worship? That a particular composer of the past (or present) had or has a defective view of liturgy, or was not a Catholic or Christian, says nothing about whether or not the music he or she has composed functions well in our liturgy. Much music of the past might well fit our liturgy – and much of it might well not – but in either case the question should be approached from the grounds of pure liturgical requirements and no other.

The impression that ritual music today consists *only of new, untraditional* music must be challenged. Ritual music today embraces, along with responsorial psalms and recent Mass settings, the congregational Gregorian Mass XVIII, a Palestrina choral Gloria or a vernacular hymn sung by congregation and choir. All of these, under given conditions, could be ritual music in the fullest sense of the term.

The notion that ritual and aesthetic principles of evaluation are in conflict with each other needs also to be confronted and dismissed. A reflection on the issues involved would surely suggest that, far from there being conflict, it is clear that beauty is a necessary element of ritual. Article 5 of *Snowbird* suggests that when the two requirements are in equilibrium there is an enrichment, which is to the ultimate enhancement of the living liturgical experience:

> The theory and practice of ritual music is often inadequately attentive to the beautiful and the artistic. It often seems to go unnoticed that aesthetically high-quality music has the ability to make rituals more powerful and more engaging. . . . We call for a further development in the concept and practice of ritual music so as to avoid utilitarian functionalism and to advance a liturgical music practice that is beautiful and artistically well formed.

If worship music is to be subservient to the requirements of ritual, then surely there are grounds for regarding music of the Roman Catholic and other Christian traditions of ages past as suitable for contemporary usage; and if the aesthetic dimension in liturgical music is affirmed as a criterion for acceptance, then it can certainly be argued that Pius X's concerns that music in worship be holy, beautiful in form, and at the service of ritual, are principles as relevant today as they were in 1903, although naturally the context and interpretation of these concerns must be modified appropriately to meet the needs of the vastly changed circumstances of contemporary liturgical requirements.

Notes

1.   See Oliver Strunk, *Source Readings in Music History* (New York: W.W. Norton & Co., 1950), pp. 64–75.
2.   James McKinnon, *Music in Early Christian Literature* (Cambridge: Cambridge University Press, 1987), pp. 49–95.
3.   See article by Stanley Sadie in *The New Grove* (London: Macmillan, 1980), XII, p. 691
4   As in *The Jerusalem Bible*, ed. by Alexander Jones (London: Darton, Longman & Todd, 1966/1979), pp. 930, 6385.
5.   Rembert Weakland, *Letter to Composers* (Milwaukee, 1980)
6.   As quoted in the *Irish Times*, 9 September 1996
7.   *Music in Catholic Worship* (Washington: Bishops' Committee on the Liturgy, National Conference of Catholic Bishops, 1972/rev. 1983), pp. 14–18.
8.   See Robert F. Hayburn, *Papal Legislation in Sacred Music 95AD to 1979AD* (Collegeville, Minnesota: The Liturgical Press, 1979)
9.   For full text see *Documents on the Liturgy 1963-1979*, ed. by ICEL (Collegeville, Minnesota: The Liturgical Press, 1982), pp. 1293–1306.
10. See Strunk, op. cit. and McKinnon, op. cit.
11. See, for example, Norman Carrell, *Bach the Borrower* (London: George Allen & Unwin, 1967), Chapters III & IV, and Karl Geringer in *The Mozart Companion,* ed. by H.C. Robbins Landon and Donald Mitchell (London: Rockliff, 1956/rev. 1964), p. 365.
12. See Carl Schalk, *Key Words in Church Music* (St Louis: Concordia, 1978)
13. Hayburn, op. cit.
14. For a full discussion on Cecilian ideals with particular reference to Ireland, see Kieran A. Daly, *Catholic Church Music in Ireland 1878–1903* (Dublin: Four Courts Press, 1995)
15. *Musicae sacrae disciplina* (1955). See Hayburn, op. cit.
16. The full translated texts of the Instruction *De musica sacra et sacra liturgia* (1958) and *Musicam sacram* (1967) may be consulted in Hayburn, op. cit.

17. *The Snowbird Statement on Catholic Liturgical Music* (Salt Lake City: The Madeleine Institute, 1995). The present author is a signatory of the statement.

18. Dom Anthony Ruff OSB of the University of Graz (Austria) and St John's Abbey, Collegeville, Minnesota, presented a paper at the September 1996 conference of the Madeleine Institute, Salt Lake City, on 'Holiness Beauty and Ritual: Pius X on Liturgical Music Revisited'. His closely argued polemic has inspired the writing of the present article. Dom Anthony is also a signatory of *The Snowbird Statement.*

19. Ruff, op. cit.

20. Ruff, op. cit.

21. For a fuller discussion of this issue, see Edward Foley, *Ritual Music: Studies in Liturgical Musicology* (Beltsville, Maryland: The Pastoral Press, 1995), pp. 89–106.

22. *Tra le Sollecitudini:* 1:23 as in Hayburn, op. cit.

Music As Therapy: The Sounds of Healing

Kaja Jensen

A FORM OF HUMAN EXPRESSION, music embodies the ambiguous: life/death, love/hate, joy/sorrow, pride/pity, the simple/the complex, the necessary/the frivolous, solidarity/solitude, humour/angst, tension/release, sound/silence. In light of this, music provides for us a tangible microcosm of the intangible. It is that which can be acquired nowhere else except through and with music. Because of this, all music exquisitely represents and in turn influences human behaviour. We would be remiss to ignore the impact of music in and on our lives, and imprudent to disregard the potential of music to act as a healing agent.

As an historical concept, music and healing have been intimately wed. From the philosophical ideas of Plato and Aristotle, both advocates of the controlled, systematic use of music to promote ethical behaviour and health, to the twentieth and twenty-first centuries, which have yielded numerous examples of the therapeutic, transforming and medicinal impact of music as well as the profession of music therapy, we discover the potential of music to act as an agent of change. The following will provide a brief illustration of the varied applications of music in a healing context.

Music, a complex (harmony, melody, rhythm), serial, communicative stimulus is present in all cultures and is a unique medium from which we gain inimitable understanding of the world around us. Not unlike Durkheim's theory of ritual, which states that religious practice creates and sustains human social structure as well as assists us in maintaining a sense of reality, the act of making, spontaneously creating or listening to music also validates social institutions, contributes to the continuity and stability of cultural norms, and transmits and represents human knowledge.[1]

Who among us has not enhanced or altered their mood by listening to a favourite musical selection? Ask yourself if you have ever put on music to make a menial task go faster or used music as a distraction while driving a familiar stretch of road. Have you ever had to turn off music because it so intruded on your ability to concentrate? Or been able to exercise longer because you were working out to the rhythm of music? What lovers among us do not have a song that embodies our sentiment and connection to each other? Have you been brought to tears or had goose bumps while singing your national anthem or church hymns? In some small measure these simple examples elucidate a broader truth. The experience of music (actively making or actively listening) has tremendous psychological and physiological effects.

Let us begin our examination of the psychological and physiological effects of music by first defining our terms and delimiting our discussion. When music is referred to it means the intentional use of organised vocal and instrumental sounds as well as silence. It is uniquely human behaviour. It includes both the acts of making and/or listening. Healing in the context of this paper refers to a continuum of becoming psychologically, physically, and/or spiritually better – getting well. From this perspective healing is a process of achieving wholeness or change, not necessarily achieving a cure. Thus, in the discussion below the use of music by an educated professional to act broadly as an agent of change and the various roles that music plays in diverse settings will be explored.

Music as an organisational/structural device?

Since the 1991 US Senate hearings on music and aging, there has been a tremendous increase in the number of music therapists employed in nursing homes and managed care facilities. Research and clinical work in the area of Alzheimer's disease (AD) has risen sharply.[2] Results from studies that examine the effects of music listening with the elderly suggest that the experience can reduce social isolation,[3] increase alertness, improve mood and enhance memory.[4] Furthermore, in a study that examined the differential effects of listening to classical music or preferred music, Gerdner[5] discovered a reduction in agitation behaviours in AD patients during and following music listening sessions.

Music therapists who use music-making interventions with AD patients have discovered an improvement in speech production,[6] increased participation between family caregivers and care receivers,[7] as well as increased social participation, improved recall, and decreased problem behaviours.[8] The above is not intended to be an exhaustive, critical review of research findings, but an overview of the healing potential of music. In my own experience, working and educating students on Alzheimer's units, nothing excites us more than observing the ability of music to evoke memories in patients who are confused, disoriented, and clearly suffering. Consider the following case example.

Case example

Two music therapy students under my supervision provided services on the Alzheimer's Unit of a managed care residential facility. As a part of the student's educational requirements they provided ten weeks of sessions. Our group sessions lasted one hour and occurred once a week. There were typically ten residents in the group.

During assessment, we observed 'typical' difficulties with relating to others, disorientation to time and place, confusion, anxiety and decline in personal hygiene. At about the fourth session, the students and I became particularly concerned with 'F.' She was especially agitated and disoriented. 'F''s daughter, who regularly participated in the music therapy session, was also distressed about her mother's agitation. In advance of the session we had decided to use familiar songs to stimulate memories of past events and promote discussion among group members. Given 'F''s current distress, we decided to use one of her preferred folk songs. The song 'Home on the Range' immediately engaged 'F', who sung along and encouraged the participation of other group members.

The song was used as an impetus for discussion. Our discussion questions centred around growing up in rural Texas. Through this discussion we discovered that 'F' grew up on a farm, had many chores, including feeding chickens, cleaning the horse stalls and milking the cows. 'F' even went on to joke about the dangers of milking.

'F''s animated participation engaged other group members as well as the students and me, who entered into appropriate discussion with 'F'. She conversed easily with us and attracted the attention of the nursing staff, who had not heard her story before. This started a lively discussion between staff and group members. 'F''s daughter, surprised at her mother's now animated and enthusiastic discourse, ended up holding her hand and reinforcing 'F''s 'on task', socially appropriate behaviour.

The experience concluded with adding new group-oriented lyrics to the familiar tune. When the session was over, 'F' easily complied with returning to her unit. She initiated discussion with her daughter, thanked the students and me, and reminded us that we'd see her next week – same time, same place! What the students and I observed was a profound change in 'Fs' affect, socialisation, and orientation to time and place. The students and I were convinced that it was the familiar song that provided the window of opportunity for reality orientation and discussion.

In the 1990s, music therapists also found an increased need for their skills in the treatment of medical conditions. Patients in medical settings have enjoyed the stimulation, emotional support, independence, stress reduction and pain relief that music can provide.[9] Stoudenmire,[10] for example, investigated the effects of muscle relaxation and relaxing music on the reduction of state and trait anxiety. Stoudenmire proposes that music be used as a temporary anxiety reduction method in instances where muscle relaxation is deemed inappropriate because of various physical ailments. Music therapy studies also cite the effect of music in pain management[11] and as an audio-analgesic for dental patients.[12]

Medical conditions often have a significant impact on both emotional and social functioning. Specifically in children, long-term hospitalisation significantly impairs cognitive and social development. Often children face developmental delays as a result of their illness or treatment.[13] Literature suggests that developmental delays may be the initial presentation of neurological dysfunction in an HIV infected child.[14]

Central nervous system involvement in HIV infected infants and toddlers most commonly produces a progressive generalised brain disease (encephalopathy) resulting in failure to attain or maintain developmental milestones. A particular feature of pediatric HIV infection is an often rapid and unpredictable change in developmental status. Often, a child presents with motor, cognitive, communication and/or social emotional delays. Pediatric HIV infection frequently results in a population of children who are either at risk for or have developmental disabilities.

While working as a research assistant in a medical school, I was able to provide music therapy services on an infant critical care unit. It just so happened that the majority of hospitalised infants and toddlers were diagnosed with HIV infection. The unit itself was arranged in typical fashion. There were about nine cribs placed along three sides of an open room surrounding a nurse's station. Typically, a television provided the only non-hospital sounds on the unit.

The apparent isolation of these children was one of the first clinical observations that challenged me as a music therapist and caused me to assess a number of their possible social/emotional needs.

First, the need for non-intrusive interaction was striking. Second, the need for nurturing and loving attention was apparent and developmentally appropriate. Finally, in order to accomplish the above, a technique and method were needed that would allow for passive physical involvement. It was with these criteria in mind that I began vocally improvising with HIV infected children. The reader is reminded that the data reported are behavioural observations and possibly confounded by personal bias. Nevertheless, although causal relationships cannot be established, behavioural changes did occur.

Case example

'B' was a thirteen-month-old, HIV infected male, hospitalised for pneumocystis carinii pneumonia (PCP). He was dehydrated, anaemic, and on a respirator. He was on commonly used medications (AZT and bactrim) for HIV infection.

When I entered the unit, he was lying on his stomach with his arms at his sides. His hands were clenched into fists and he was engaged in seemingly non-purposeful, non-expressive monotone crying. The unit staff reports indicated that he was non-interactive and continually vocalised in a stereotypical manner.

In an attempt to establish eye contact with 'B', I approached the crib, leaned inside and vocalised a greeting. He was unresponsive to this, at which point I began singing his name. I matched his pith and used an improvised melody of minor thirds. Within approximately seven seconds, 'B' stopped vocalising, rotated his head toward me, and established eye contact with me. He maintained eye contact with me as I improvised for close to five seconds then resumed the monotone vocalising. This cycle continued for about six minutes when I noticed that 'B' had opened his hands. Since my hand was within about three inches of his I responded by stroking his little finger. He grasped my finger and continued the stereotypical vocalising. Although I continued to vocally improvise in an attempt to engage him in vocal play, he persisted with the monotone vocalising, stopping only to establish and maintain eye contact with me for brief periods. The vocal improvisation session lasted fifteen minutes. He established eye contact with me six times, each time maintaining eye contact for 3–15 seconds. In total, based on behavioural observation, 'B' initiated and maintained eye contact for about 3 per cent of the entire session. It was a modest but noteworthy exchange.

Case example
Visit 1: 'S' was a twenty-three-month-old HIV infected female. She was hospitalised with malnutrition, fever, encephalopathy, cardiomyopathy, anaemia, herpes, and oral thrush. She was on standard medications for HIV infection and accompanying syndromes.

At the onset of the session 'S' appeared agitated. She was grinding her teeth and scratching her ears and head. Her crib was placed near the unit door, but she did not seem to notice my entrance nor other traffic, in or out of the unit. When I approached the crib I attempted to represent her teeth-grinding through vocal improvisations. She immediately stopped, dropped her hands to her side, opened her mouth, and established eye contact with me. I continued to vocalise but in a legato fashion, specifically humming, and on 'ah'. I used primarily a dorian scale, my aim being to produce a warm, soothing vocal sound. 'S' appeared to habituate to my vocalisations and returned to grinding her teeth. I responded by vocalising her name using a major tonality, closed, nasal vowel sounds and dance-like rhythms. Rhythmically, I tried to collaborate with the teeth grinding sounds she was producing. She responded again by establishing and maintaining eye contact with me.

This process continued for fifteen minutes, at which point she reached out to me. She had not been grinding her teeth for about three minutes prior to this. I picked her up, sat in a rocking chair and continued to vocally improvise, varying the vowel sounds, tonality, and rhythmic phrasing. Within a few minutes I stopped vocalising and rocking. She, much to my surprise as well as to the staff in the room, turned her head, looked up at me and clearly vocalised a descending minor third on 'ah'. We continued the cause and effect game for about ten minutes. Throughout the vocal play she gradually made longer phrases, imitating the melodic contour and vowel sounds I was making.

Our game-playing attracted the attention of an ambulatory toddler in the nursery. 'S' noticed his presence and responded by establishing eye contact with him, reaching out for him, and vocalising to him. 'S''s inclusion of the toddler was a moving experience for me as well as the unit staff. The vocal improvisation session lasted approximately forty minutes. 'S''s initial self-absorbed, isolated behaviour was facilitated through vocal improvisation towards self-initiated social interaction.

Visit 2. Two days later I attempted to see 'S' again. When I entered the nursery 'S' was lying on her back. Her hands were bandaged to prevent self-injury through scratching. This time she was not grinding her teeth. I approached the crib, vocalising her name as I moved toward her. She immediately acknowledged my presence through eye contact and spontaneous vocalisations. I leaned inside the crib, placing my arm within her reach and perpendicular to her body. We engaged in vocal play using grunts, alternating guttural 'g' and 'ah' sounds. Rhythmically, phrases varied. She used melodic phrases that were twenty seconds in length and were about twice as long as phrases in the previous session. We played an altered version of the cause and effect game, in which 'S' would reach out her hand to touch my face when I stopped singing. At one point in our twenty-minute session, I sang an interval that was uncharacteristically dissonant (M7). This seemed to surprise 'S' and she laughed. Her laughter captured the attention of her father and the staff on the unit. The father with tears in his eyes revealed that he had never before heard his daughter laugh. The unit staff, now engaged with 'S', proceeded to call her name and talk to her. Once again it seemed as though vocal improvisation was a catalyst from which 'S' achieved social interaction.

These case examples represent an average sample of about twenty sessions with six HIV infected children. Each one was chosen because it represented an average vocal improvisation session. An overview of the session notes revealed that child responses included: (a) vocalising, (b) establishing and maintaining eye contact, (c) initiating physical contact, and/or (d) sleeping. All responses seemed directly related to vocal improvisation, which provided developmentally appropriate stimulation and encouraged the children to interact with and respond to their environment.

What is it about music that engaged these infants? The answer is not arrived at easily. What does seem clear is that music seems to promote learning and assist in the process of attaining or maintaining developmental milestones. It appears as if there is information, not explicit information as in lyrics, but implicit information that is contained in and supplied through music. Social information is one type of information commonly transmitted in a musical context.

In various settings, music functions as a cohesion builder and social metaphor. For example in church, congregation singing can promote the social integration of the community. At a sporting event, the team band and team songs promote an atmosphere of comradeship. Music reminds us of and engages us in a shared goal, a common purpose. It is unifying. For people who are in crisis or have a mental or physical disability, the simple act of socialising, something most of us take for granted, becomes an insurmountable hurdle. Additionally, people who face life challenges may also have difficulty expressing their thoughts and feelings. The inability to express oneself often exaggerates or complicates a psychological or medical condition.

Music as emotionally evocative

The crisis surrounding AIDS has led psychological researchers and medical researchers to search for treatment strategies. The mass hysteria provoked by preliminary and unsubstantiated information on AIDS has contributed to the irrational fears and prejudice that have encouraged an unbearable social climate for patients. It is within this framework that researchers have insisted that psychosocial research is essential for treating AIDS,[15] helping AIDS patients in crisis,[16] and assisting volunteers who treat persons with AIDS.[17] Price, Omizo, and Hammett[18] directly challenge counsellors to educate their patients on topics such as nutrition, stress management, relaxation techniques, and coping through visual imagery.

The following study was designed to examine the question: How does the combined use of music and visualisation as compared to traditional verbal psychotherapy effect psychotherapeutic outcome on a person with AIDS? Bonny and Pahnke[19] state five ways in which music can complement therapeutic objectives:

1. It helps the patient relinquish usual controls and more fully enter his inner world of experience.
2. It facilitates the release of intense emotionality.
3. It contributes towards a peak experience.
4. It provides continuity in an experience of timelessness.
5. It directs and structures the experience.

Volunteer participants were randomly assigned to a music and visualisation group. Verbal counselling participants volunteered and were seen on a first-come, first-serve basis. Participants in both groups were seen individually once a week for six sessions. The Gottschalk-Gleser Content Analysis Anxiety Scale was used on patient verbalisations across sessions.

All participants were male, ranging in age from twenty-eight to forty-four, with a mean age of thirty-seven. Seven participants were diagnosed with HIV infection and one participant was diagnosed with AIDS. All participants claimed to be exclusively gay. Verbal counselling group members had been seen in treatment prior to the onset of this investigation. The number of prior verbal treatment sessions ranged from eight to thirty-two, with a mean of seventeen. Music and visualisation group members were not seen in music and visualisation treatment sessions prior to the onset of this investigation.

The music consisted of tape recordings of various instrumental and vocal selections. Tape selection was dependent on my clinical judgment and participant preference. The majority of music selections were organised and compiled on cassette tape by Helen Bonny and can be found in her 1978 monograph #2 on guided imagery and music.[20] In a 1976 paper she states: The variables within the music that seemed to carry the strongest implications for guided imagery and music were pitch, rhythm and tempo, vocal and instrumental, melody (linear line) and harmony, timbre (colour), and form.[21]

The music selected for this project followed similar guidelines: for example, if my perception of participant needs suggested confrontation, musical selections with movement, drive, and bombastic sequences were deemed appropriate. Alternately, music selections less demanding, more predictable and stable, were used to promote a feeling of safety.

Subjective anxiety state was measured with the Gottschalk-Gleser Content Analysis Anxiety Scale.[22] Each session, the first 150–250 words were used per participant for the purpose of content analysis. Participant verbalisations were recorded on video tape or mini cassette tape during the verbal counselling sessions and by hand, in a session log, during the music and visualisation sessions.

Content analysis of verbal behaviour is a research technique for making inferences. This is accomplished by systematically and objectively identifying specified characteristics in spoken or written language. Content analytic procedures are designed to specify judgmental processes and transform intuitive evaluations into explicit rules by developing categories of speech units

The Gottschalk-Gleser content analysis method takes into consideration contextual aspects of the message, its coding unit being the grammatical clause as established by a coder. It relies on frequency counts of relevant categories modified by weighting. Weight depends on the proximity to a predefined construct and personal involvement of the speaker.

The anxiety scale is sub-divided into six forms. This includes death, mutilation, separation, guilt, shame and diffuse or nonspecific anxiety. Further details of the construct 'anxiety,' the assumptions underlying the scale, and a review of reliability, validity and normative data are detailed in Gottschalk and Gleser.[23]

All participants were seen, by either myself or a research associate, in individual sessions. Each music and visualisation participant underwent an orientation to the Somatron and to the available tape recordings, during which I explained in detail how music therapy procedures were to be used throughout the participant's participation. I kept an account of each treatment session as a session log and included the date, the musical selections chosen, participant verbalisations, researcher verbalisations, researcher observations, and recommendations for the following session. The format for the music and visualisation treatment sessions was as follows.

Each session began with a warm-up phase. During this phase I asked each participant to participate in breathing exercises, progressive muscle relaxation, and body part visualisation. This process continued while I provided the musical selection. While the music played, the participant was asked to verbalise any thoughts, feelings, ideas, images and/or sensations. I gradually facilitated the sessions toward the active phase, where the participant was asked to perceive (visually and/or kinesthetically) the disease process as it was occurring in his/her body. The content of this phase was patient-centred or focused on immediate patient concerns. Once this was accomplished the participant was asked to visualise producing healthy cells to engage in combat with and destroy the diseased cells. When the participant was able to perceive a successful battle, he/she was asked to 'symbolically' dispose of the battle casualties. Upon successful completion of the above, participants were asked to imagine themselves as healthy individuals fulfilling future life goals. Each session concluded with a closure phase, the content of which was based on session information. The session format varied per participant and per session. The phases were not mutually exclusive; session content was based on participant output. The above was an overall treatment guide, subject to alteration based on patient needs.

Results yielded a statistically significant increase in the expression of anxiety in the music and visualisation sessions compared to the verbal psychotherapy session during week two and week five. Although not statistically significant, music and visualisation anxiety scores were higher than verbal counselling anxiety scores for all sessions except for session six.

Of clinical interest is the amount of information expressed during both interventions. The verbal counselling (VC) participants spoke approximately six times more often (based on word frequency counts) than music and visualisation (MV) group members. However, the overall number of codable clauses for the construct anxiety differed considerably between groups. The VC group contained twenty-six codable clauses, while the MV group contained seventy-two codable clauses.

Much of the VC group 'verbalising time' was spent providing historical narratives of specific events, such as trips taken, conversations held, meetings attended, and the like. MV group members spoke less and spoke of immediate experience. Yalom[24] insists that therapy that 'hopes to effect extensive and enduring behavioral and characterological change . . . strongly emphasizes the importance of the here-and-now experience'. Perhaps the ahistoric thrust of the MV group sessions led to anxiety-provoking experience.

Another clinically significant result is the context in which the anxiety is being generated. The majority of codable clauses in the MV group fell into the anxiety subtype death (32%) followed by the anxiety subtype guilt (22%). However, the majority of codable clauses in the VC group fell into the diffuse or nonspecific anxiety subtype (35%) followed by the subtype guilt (19%). Gottschalk, Winget, and Gleser utilise the subtype diffuse or nonspecific anxiety when it is impossible to distinguish the type of anxiety being expressed.[25] Although an equally potent source of anxiety, perhaps the historic orientation of the VC group led to the abundance of diffuse anxiety statements.

The predominance of the anxiety subtype death suggests immediate existential sentiment expression in the MV group. Yalom insists that existential factors such as death, freedom, isolation, and life-purpose play an important but generally unrecognisable role in psychotherapy. Yalom further explains that an important concept in existential therapy is that human beings may relate to ultimate concerns of existence in two possible modes – forgetfulness of being and mindfulness of being. Yalom states:

> Being aware of one's self-creation in the authentic state of mindfulness of being provides one with the power to change. . . . It was clear to me that the members . . . who plunged most deeply into themselves, who confronted their fate most openly and resolutely, passed into a mode of existence that was richer.[26]

It is plausible that the music and visualisation group experienced a direct expression of their terminal condition – mindfulness of being, while the verbal counselling group tended toward denial – forgetfulness of being. By directly experiencing, through and with the music, the emotions associated with their illness, transcending the experience and integrating the experience, the music and visualisation here-and-now focus seems to have led to interpersonal learning, intrapersonal learning, and the development of coping strategies.[27] The ability of music to evoke emotion is not a novel idea. However, using this common response to music for therapeutic transformation may seem foreign to some. Consider the following case example.

Case example

While working as a music therapist, I provided services to a single mother (twenty-eight years old), 'M'. She was diagnosed with AIDS, had several bouts of pneumonia and been hospitalised several times. 'M' herself was raised by a single mother (now deceased), who because of work and an alcohol problem was emotionally unavailable to 'M'. 'M''s father had left home when she was a toddler, never to be seen again. As 'M' prepared for the end of her life it was clear that she had unfinished business with her own upbringing, which was affecting her current relationship with her own children and her ability to cope with her diagnosis.

She was the mother of three children, the youngest of whom was diagnosed with HIV infection and was failing to thrive. She was angry, having trouble sleeping, and worried about her future and the future of her children. She was depressed. She was referred to music therapy to address her insomnia and existential concerns. We met once a week for six months.

At approximately week 7, I found myself at a loss as to how to proceed. I had tried to engage her in music, relaxation, and visualisation (a technique that had worked well in addressing similar client needs in my past experience), lyric substitution (putting her words to familiar melodies), performing her preferred music, and writing songs. Nothing worked.

At home one evening after a session with 'M' I found myself summarising my observations of 'M' in a song. The lyrics to the song I wrote are as follows

> Forgiveness
> F#m7   G#m7/E
> A whole lifetime of feeling passed before my eyes
> F#m7   G#m7/E
> The heavens opened up and cried
> Adom7   G3m7 Gdom7
> A sky consumed with grieving for an innocent child
> (Bridge)
> It's funny what a word can do
> It's simple what a word can do
> It's horrid what a word can do
> It's simple what a word can do
>
> An all-consuming sorrow passed before my eyes
> A pain so deep it dropped me to my knees
> There is no comfort found within another man's fight
> (Bridge)
>
> (Chorus)
> Can you forgive her?
> Forgive him?

Forgive them?
Forgive me?
This living
(3 additional verses dealing with grief, survival, and hope)

At our next meeting I told 'M' I had written her a song and asked her if I could play it. She agreed. I began to sing and play. When I got to the chorus, 'M' was visibly moved. She had started to cry, her head bent. By the end of the song 'M' was sobbing and rocking herself gently. I continued to hum the melody until her sobbing subsided. She asked me if I would teach her the song. Of course I agreed. We sang the song together a number of times, her voice stronger and more confident with each rendition. Finally, we stopped. She told me that although she never realised it until this moment she had always considered herself a mistake. After all, if her own mother paid no attention to her, why was she here? She confessed that on some level she didn't believe she deserved to live. She didn't want to end her life, but felt she should apologise for her very existence. She also confessed ambiguous feelings about her mother. She desperately wanted her mother's love and attention, but also felt betrayed, angry and hurt.

This 'song' session was a turning point in 'M''s work with me. She developed insight into her destructive behaviour. She realised how important it was for her to forgive herself, her mother and absentee father. She also realised that she could provide herself with the nurturing her mother never could. She was able to make some life decisions that heretofore she had been unable to confront. She enrolled in college classes. She moved into a home that more readily accommodated herself and her children. She also started parenting classes to avoid making the same mistakes with her own children. What was it in the music that made these feelings surface? What was it about a musical context that made her feelings tolerable and accessible? What was it about the music that offered her insight into her own thoughts, feelings, and experiences?

Conclusion
The above in no way addresses all the areas where music is used to achieve therapeutic outcomes. Although brief, it seems obvious from

the above that music stimulates us physiologically, contains and supports us psychologically, influences us cognitively, motivates us socially, accesses us emotionally, inspires, transforms, and challenges us spiritually. It is hoped that the above discussion will entice readers to investigate, in greater depth, the healing potential of music.

Notes

1.   E. Durkheim, *The elementary forms of the religious life* (New York: Collier, 1961)

R.E. Radocy and J.D. Boyle, *Psychological foundations of musical behavior*, 3rd edn (Springfield, IL: Charles C. Thomas, 1997)

H. Gardner, *Art, mind, and brain: A cognitive approach to creativity* (New York: Basic Books, 1982)

S. Langer, *Philosophy in a new key* (Cambridge, Mass.: Harvard University Press, 1942)

T.J. Scheff, *Catharsis in healing, ritual, and drama* (Los Angeles: University of California Press, 1979)

A.P. Merriam, *The Anthropology of Music* (Evanston, Il: Northwestern University Press, 1964)

M. Kaplan, *The Arts: A Social Perspective* (Rutherford, NJ: Fairleigh Dickinson University Press, 1990)

2.   L.A. Gerdner, 'Effects of individualized versus classical "relaxation" music on the frequency of agitation in elderly persons with Alzheimer's disease and related disorders', *International Psychogeriatrics,* 12 (2000), 49–65.

M. Brotons, S.M. Koger and P. Pickett-Cooper, 'Music and dementias: A review of the literature: Erratum', *Journal of Music Therapy,* 36 (1999), 16–21.

D. Aldridge, 'Music therapy and the treatment of Alzheimer's disease', *Clinical Gerentologist,* 16 (1995), 41–57.

A. Clair, *Therapeutic Uses of Music With Older Adults* (Baltimore, MD: Health Professions Press, 1996)

3.   Aldridge, op. cit.

4.   T.R. Lord and J.E. Garner 'Effects of music on alzheimer's patients', *Perceptual and Motor Skills,* 76 (1993), 451–455.

5.   Gerdner, op. cit.

6.   Aldridge, op. cit.

7.   A. Clair, 'The effects of music therapy on interactions between family caregivers and their care receivers with late stage dementia', *Journal of Music Therapy,* 34 (1997), 148–164.

8.   Brotons, Koger and Pickett-Cooper, op. cit.

9. C.D. Marantod, ed., *Applications of Music in Medicine* (Washington DC: NAMT, 1991)

10. J. Stoudenmire, 'A comparison of muscle relaxation training and music in the reduction of state and trait anxiety', *Journal of Clinical Psychology,* 31 (1975), 490–492.

11. S.B. Hanser, S.C. Larson and A.S. O'Connell, 'The effect of music on relaxation of expectant mothers during labor', *Journal of Music Therapy,* 20 (1983), 50–58.
    M.E., Clark, R.R. McCorkle and S.B. Williams, 'Music-therapy-assisted labor and delivery', *Journal of Music Therapy* 18 (1981), 88–109.

12. S.B. Hanser, P. Martin, and K. Bradstreet, 'The effect of music on relaxation of dental patients', Paper presented at the meeting of the National Association of Music Therapy, Baltimore, MD (November, 1982).

13. J. Barrickman, 'A developmental music therapy approach for preschool hospitalized children', *Music Therapy Perspectives,* 7 (1989), 10–16.
    W.B. Davis, K.E. Gfeller, and M.H. Thaut, *An Introduction to Music Therapy: Theory and Practice* (Boston: McGraw-Hill College, 1999)

14. J.F. Seidel, J.M. Seibert, G. Scott, A. Garcia, G. DeGraff, B. Loyd, K.L. Jensen, S. Perez, *Pediatric HIV infection: Guidelines for psychosocial case management,* Manuscript funded by the Florida Developmental Disabilities Planning Council, 1992.

15. T.J. Coates, L. Temoshok and J. Mandel, 'Psychosocial research is essential to understanding and treating AIDS', *American Psychologist,* 39 (1984), 1309–1314.

16. D.J. Lopez and G.S. Getzel, 'Helping gay AIDS patients in crisis: social casework', *Journal of Contemporary Social Work,* 65 (1984), 387–394.
    W.F. Batchelor, 'AIDS: A public health and psychological emergency', *American Psychologist,* 39 (1984), 1279–1284.
    S. Namir, D.L. Wolcott, I.F. Fauzy and M.J. Alumbaugh, 'Coping with AIDS: Psychological and health implications', *Journal of Applied Social Psychology,* 17 (1987), 309–328.

17. Lopez and Getzel, op. cit.
    M. Bremmer and L.B. Brown, 'Learning to care for clients with AIDS – the practicum controversy', *Nursing and Health Care,* 7 (1986), 251–253.

18. R.E. Price, M.M. Omizo and V.L. Hammett, 'Counseling clients with AIDS', *Journal of Counseling and Development,* 65 (1986), 96–97.

19. H.L. Bonny and W.N. Pahnke, 'The use of music in psychedelic (LSD) psychotherapy', *Journal of Music Therapy,* 9 (1982), 65–87.

20. H.L. Bonny, *The role of taped music programs in the GIM process: GIM monograph #2* (Baltimore, MD: ICM Books, 1978).

21.   H.L. Bonny, *Music and psychotherapy*, Unpublished doctoral dissertation, The Union of Experimenting Colleges and Universities, Baltimore, Maryland (1976).

22.   L.A. Gottschalk, C.N. Winget, and G.C. Gleser, *Manual of instructions using the gottschalk-gleser content analysis scales: anxiety, hostility and social alienation-personal disorganization* (Los Angeles: University of California Press, 1969)

23.   L.A. Gottschalk and G.C. Gleser, *The measurement of psychological states through the content analysis of verbal behavior* (Los Angeles: University of California Press, 1969)

24.   I.D. Yalom, *The theory and practice of group psychotherapy*, 3rd edn (New York: Basic Books, 1985)

25.   Gottschalk, Winget, and Gleser, op. cit., p.52.

26.   Yalom, op. cit., pp. 98, 100.

27.   Yalom, op. cit.
      Price, Omizo and Hammett, 'Counseling clients with AIDS', *Journal of Counseling and Development*, 65 (1986), 96–97.